Stefanie Schmaus

A Brand Identity for the Frisian Wadden Sea

Destination Branding on the Basis of Destination Image Analysis

Schriftenreihe der School of International Business
Internationaler Studiengang für Tourismusmanagement (ISTM)

Herausgegeben von Felix Bernhard Herle

Band 10

SCHRIFTENREIHE DER SCHOOL OF INTERNATIONAL BUSINESS
Internationaler Studiengang für Tourismusmanagement (ISTM)

Herausgegeben von Felix Bernhard Herle

ISSN 1863-9798

2 *Stefanie Kranawetter und Ivonne Mühlner*
Erfolgreiches Krisenmanagement für Reiseveranstalter
Ein Handbuch für plötzlich auftretende Krisen im Tourismus
ISBN 978-3-89821-835-1

3 *Angela Bergner*
Tourismus als Mittel zur Armutsminderung in Nepal
Das "Tourism for Rural Poverty Alleviation Programme" (TRPAP)
ISBN 978-3-89821-853-5

4 *Felix Bernhard Herle*
Strategische Planung grenzenloser Destinationen
Vertikale und branchenübergreifende Erweiterung Touristischer Regionen
ISBN 978-3-89821-908-2

5 *Birte Heidbreder*
Gütesiegel zur Einflussnahme auf die touristische Entwicklung einer Destination
Erfolgsanalyse des CST Costa Ricas für nachhaltigen Tourismus
ISBN 978-3-89821-986-0

6 *Linda von Nerée*
Das touristische Potential Hamburgs für chinesische Europa-Reisende
Eine Bestandsanalyse mit konkreten Veränderungsvorschlägen
ISBN 978-3-89821-780-4

7 *Joana Heinemann*
Mountainbike-Tourismus im Wettbewerb
Zielgruppenorientierte Optimierung von Packages im Destinationsmarketing
ISBN 978-3-8382-0167-2

8 *Tina Böttinger*
Die Entwicklung der Erlebnisorientierung
Status quo und Perspektiven in der Kreuzfahrt- und Themenparkbranche
ISBN 978-3-8382-0259-4

9 *Moritz Busch*
Kooperationspotenziale von Lufthansa und Germanwings aus Konsumentenperspektive
Eine Untersuchung zu Einflussfaktoren auf die konsumentenperspektivische Akzeptanz von Kooperationen konträrer Geschäftsmodelle
ISBN 978-3-8382-0456-7

10 *Stefanie Schmaus*
A Brand Identity for the Frisian Wadden Sea
Destination Branding on the Basis of Destination Image Analysis
ISBN 978-3-8382-0490-1

Stefanie Schmaus

A BRAND IDENTITY FOR THE FRISIAN WADDEN SEA

Destination Branding on the Basis
of Destination Image Analysis

Schriftenreihe der School of International Business
Internationaler Studiengang für Tourismusmanagement (ISTM)

Herausgegeben von Felix Bernhard Herle

Band 10

ibidem-Verlag
Stuttgart

Bibliografische Information der Deutschen Nationalbibliothek
Die Deutsche Nationalbibliothek verzeichnet diese Publikation in der Deutschen Nationalbibliografie; detaillierte bibliografische Daten sind im Internet über http://dnb.d-nb.de abrufbar.

Bibliographic information published by the Deutsche Nationalbibliothek
Die Deutsche Nationalbibliothek lists this publication in the Deutsche Nationalbibliografie; detailed bibliographic data are available in the Internet at http://dnb.d-nb.de.

Cover picture: © Anja Semling / PIXELIO

∞

Gedruckt auf alterungsbeständigem, säurefreien Papier
Printed on acid-free paper

ISSN: 1863-9798

ISBN-13: 978-3-8382-0490-1

Printed in Germany

Vorwort

Die Hochschule Bremen ist bereits seit Jahrzehnten eine international sehr gut vernetzte und anerkannte große Fachhochschule in Deutschland. So landeten beim aktuellen Hochschulranking des Centrums für Hochschulentwicklung (CHE) mit den Internationalen Studiengängen Wirtschaftsingenieurwesen und Fachjournalistik sowie dem Studiengang Betriebswirtschaftslehre gleich drei von vier untersuchten Fächern der Hochschule Bremen in der Kategorie internationale Ausrichtung in der Spitzengruppe. Die Hochschule Bremen galt stets als Vorreiterin für wesentliche innovative Entwicklungen. Mit der Verleihung des „Best Practice Award" des CHE, des „Marketingpreises" des DAAD und der Auszeichnung als „Reformhochschule" durch den Stifterverband ist dies angemessen und öffentlich gewürdigt worden.

Diese herausgehobene Stellung zu erhalten und weiter auszubauen ist natürlich eine wesentliche Triebfeder, sich Entwicklungen zeitgemäß anzupassen. Deshalb wurde in der Hochschule Bremen in den letzten Jahren eine Reihe tiefgreifender Veränderungen initiiert, angefangen bei der Umstellung auf das Bachelor-/Mastersystem über die Reformierung bestehender und die Einrichtung neuer Studienprogramme bis hin zur Reorganisation der 9 Fachbereiche und ihrer Zusammenfassung zu 5 Fakultäten.

Bei all diesen Entwicklungsprozessen haben die Fachbereiche „Nautik und Internationale Wirtschaft/School of International Business (FB 6)" sowie „Wirtschaft (FB 9)" eine besondere Rolle in der Hochschule Bremen gespielt. Von Beginn an galt die Internationalisierung als das wesentliche Markenzeichen beider Fachbereiche. Seit März 2008 sind beide Fachbereiche zur Fakultät Wirtschaftswissenschaften fusioniert. Die Bezeichnung „School of International Business (SIB)" aus dem ehemaligen FB 6 wurde dabei auch für die neue Fakultät als bereits etablierter Markenname beibehalten, nicht zuletzt, um die besondere Bedeutung der Internationalität in der Fakultät zu unterstreichen.

Mit nunmehr über 3200 Studierenden prägt diese große Fakultät natürlich das Profil der Hochschule Bremen deutlich: Von den elf Bachelorstudiengängen und zehn Masterstudiengängen (davon drei als konsekutive Masterstudiengänge der Fakultät bzw. in Verbindung mit der Fakultät Gesellschaftswissenschaften) sind nahezu 90 % internationalisiert, zum großen Teil mit einem verpflichtenden Auslandsaufenthalt, einem erheblichen Anteil curricular verankerter englischsprachiger Lehrveranstaltungen, einer intensiven interkulturellen Vorbereitung auf Auslandsaufenthalte und einer multikulturellen Lehr- und Lernatmosphäre, die durch ca. 200 internationale Gaststudierende (Incomings) und viele Lehrende von internationalen Partnereinrichtungen geprägt ist. Die Fakultät unterhält ca. 80 Auslandskooperationen weltweit, die von ca. 500 Studierenden (Outgoings) für das Auslandsstudium/Auslandspraktikum genutzt werden.

Mit dem jährlichen SIB-Kongress bietet die Fakultät einer breiten Öffentlichkeit die Möglichkeit, sich intensiv mit den Leistungen der Fakultät vertraut zu machen und Studierende wie Lehrende kennen zu lernen.

In diesem Sinne ist auch der nun vorliegende neue Band der Schriftenreihe der School of International Business (in Kooperation mit dem ***ibidem***-Verlag) als Aufforderung zu verstehen, sich mit ausgewählten Beiträgen unserer Lehrenden und Absolventen auseinander zu setzen.

Ich wünsche unseren Leserinnen und Lesern viel Freude bei der Lektüre und bin sicher, dass Sie sich von der Qualität unserer Fakultät auch auf diesem Wege überzeugen können.

Prof. Dr. Dietwart Runte
Dekan der School of International Business/Fakultät Wirtschaftswissenschaften

"The creation of the world did not take place once and for all time, but takes place every day."

Samuel Beckett, *Proust*

Acknowledgement

I would like to give sincere thanks to my supervisor Prof. Dr. Herle for supporting and guiding me during the entire research process and encouraging me to consider new perspectives and ideas.

I thank Albert Postma from the European Tourism Futures Institute for commissioning this study and providing many valuable pieces of advice.

Many thanks to Katrin Nissel for assuming the role of the second examiner and helping out with the registration while I was abroad.

I am grateful to my parents for supporting me throughout my entire education and to Artur for inspiring me in so many ways.

Abstract

Hunt (1975) argues that the destination image is essential for the success of a destination. Therefore, destination images constitute an important tool for the planning of tourism development. Moreover, destination branding can influence the destination image and elicit positive behavioural intentions (UNWTO 2009). The linkage between destination image and destination branding exists in the brand identity, since it yields the core elements of the brand which are reflected in the brand associations (Aaker 1991; Cai 2002; UNWTO 2009). Given that the brand identity is based on these associations, the destination image held by the target market is a valuable source of information for the identity development (UNWTO 2009). For this reason, the destination image of the Frisian Wadden Sea was chosen as central object of investigation and basis for the development of a brand identity for this destination. The Frisian Wadden Sea is a region in the North-Western Netherlands that encompasses unique natural assets in the form of tidal mudflats. Furthermore, the target market for the destination brand is the German population aged 18 and older, since Germany comprises the most important source market of incoming visitors to the destination (Statistics Netherlands 2012). A survey examining the destination image held by the German population was conducted and the destination associations drawn from these results were organised in the six-level brand pyramid, thus revealing the brand identity.

Contents

Index of figures and tables

Abbreviations

approx.	approximately
BC	before Christ
°C	degree Celsius
e.g.	example given
et al.	and others
etc.	etcetera
i.e.	for example
km	kilometre
m	metre
mill.	million
mm	millimetre
N	metres above sea level
n.a.	non-available

1 Introduction

In today´s globalized world, leisure tourism is an important reason for people to visit places other than their place of residence. The volume of travelers has increased highly over the last 20 years, from 435 mill. in 1990 to 940 mill. in 2010 (UNWTO 2011). Yet, the reasons why tourists choose to visit certain destinations are more complex (Mansfeld 1992). Destination selection has become an important lifestyle indicator, reflecting the visitors´ motivations and self-image (Sirgy and Su 2000; Morgan, Pritchard et al. 2004). Since the destination market in an increasingly internationalized world offers a plentitude of options and competition is high, travellers can choose from a wide range of places to visit (Morgan, Pritchard et al. 2004; UNWTO 2009). However, the *World Tourism Organisation* (*UNWTO*) (2011) predicts, that until 2020 the majority of tourists will still travel within their own region. Hence, there are opportunities for destinations to attract target markets that are geographically close. The challenge every destination faces is to convince potential tourists that the experience at the destination will satisfy their motivations and provide them with the benefits sought. Thus, there is a need to credibly communicate what the destination stands for and this can be achieved through branding (UNWTO 2009). How a destination is perceived by non-visitors and actual tourists constitutes an important indicator for its marketing strategy and brand building (Cai 2002; UNWTO 2009). The research that this study is an account of, has investigated the potential for the development of a destination brand identity on the basis of the destination image held by its most important international source market. Its relevance consists in the practical use for the Frisian Wadden Sea region by providing insights to the perceived destination image and supporting the branding process. This is particularly significant when considering that there are various national and international competitors that have already developed a destination brand such as the German brand “die Nordsee” for Lower Saxony´s Wadden Sea coast (Die Nordsee GmbH n.a.).

This study is organised in nine chapters which encompass an introduction to the research project, an overview over the research problem, aims and objectives and research questions. In continuation the theoretical background to the research is laid out. Subsequently an overview and a summary of the research design and findings from both secondary and primary analyse are provided. Finally, the research results are discussed and applied in the form of recommendations for brand identity development. The study is completed with a conclusion and an outlook.

2 The destination image of the Frisian Wadden Sea held by the German source market

The Frisian Wadden Sea area constituted the central object of investigation for this research. Thereby, the perspective of potential and actual visitors was chosen to determine how the destination could be successfully promoted on the key source market Germany. In the following the problem background and argumentation for this approach are depicted.

2.1 Problem statement

With 679,200 visitors in 2010, the province Friesland in the Netherlands is a popular Dutch holiday destination (Statistics Netherlands 2012). Particularly the Frisian coastline along the Wadden Sea offers many opportunities for coastal tourism. However, the share of 19.9% international tourists indicates that the market is mainly domestically oriented (Statistics Netherlands 2012). In order to ensure long-term competitive ability and to balance uncertainties arising from a unidirectional focus on the domestic market, it is recommendable to attract more international tourists to the Frisian Wadden Sea. Since this issue is not restricted to the Frisian Wadden Sea region, but applies to the entire Northern Netherlands, the Chamber of Commerce for the Northern Netherlands (*Kamer van Koophandel Noord Nederland*) has commissioned the *European Tourism Futures Institute* (*ETFI*) of the *Stenden University of Applied Sciences* with a project to enhance international arrivals in the Northern Netherlands including the provinces Friesland, Groningen and Drenthe.

As known from tourism research, the image of a destination is an important pull factor for potential tourists, heavily influencing their choice of destination. Therefore, projecting a positive image can successfully distinguish destinations from its competitors and increase the likelihood of visitation among potential tourists (Fakeye and Crompton 1991; Baloglu and McCleary 1999; Tasci, Gartner et al. 2007). Hence, in order to increase the attractiveness of the destination and enhance international visitor arrivals, firstly the current destination image needs to be assessed as a basis for further planning and measures. However, so far little research on the destination image of the Northern Netherlands and the Frisian Wadden Sea in particular has been conducted, especially among international tourists. For this reason, this bachelor research project commissioned by the *ETFI* examined the destination image of the Wadden Sea in Friesland and discusses implications for the positioning and promotion of the destination in the form of brand development. The focus is on potential and actual German tourists, since this source market accounted for 86.9% of all international tourism in Friesland in 2010 and this trend is estimated to continue over the next decade (NBTC 2008; Statistics Netherlands 2012). Drawing from the research findings, suggestions for attractive and strong brand associations are outlined and justified. Furthermore, recommendations for the development of a destination brand identity for the Frisian Wadden Sea in reference to the current destination image are given as an outcome of the project. Finally, research implications and limitations as fell challenges for further actions are determined.

2.2 Aims and objectives

The overall aim of this bachelor research project was to give recommendations for the development of a destination brand for the Frisian Wadden Sea area, based on the destination image held by the German source market. Therefore, the first objective was to identify and describe the current destination image of the Frisian Wadden Sea area among potential and actual German tourists. Thus, cognitive, affective, unique and holistic image components needed to be determined. Secondly, possible brand associations were deduced from the conclusions of the image analysis. In continuation, those findings were used to develop recommendations for the creation of a destination brand identity for the Frisian Wadden Sea that appeals to German tourists.

2. 3 Research questions

According to the objectives stated above, the following general research questions have been identified:

- What is the destination image of the Frisian Wadden Sea among actual and potential German tourists?

- How can this current image be used to increase the destination's attractiveness among German tourists?

More specifically, the subsequent questions were investigated:

- What are elements of the destination image with regards to cognitive, affective, unique and holistic components?

- What are differences in the destination image of potential and actual visitors?

- What are implications of the destination image for possible brand associations?

- How can the identified destination image and brand associations be used for the development of a brand identity?

3 Theoretical background

To answer the previously depicted research questions a thorough understanding of the underlying constructs destination image and destination branding as well as the area to be investigated, namely the Frisian Wadden Sea, is indispensable. Therefore, this theoretical background is provided in the form of a literature review and an area description.

3.1 The Frisian Wadden Sea area

The Frisian Wadden Sea is located in the North-West of the Netherlands in the province Friesland. The area is bordered by the Afsluitdijk in the South and the Lauwersmeer in the North. The latitude ranges from 53° 4' to 53° 30' North while the longitude coordinates are 5° 25' to 6° 16' East (n.a. 2012). The Wadden Sea forms part of the greater North Sea and has a total size of 14,700 km^2 spreading over the countries Denmark, Germany and the Netherlands (CWSS 2008). The Frisian Wadden Sea of the Netherlands belongs to the sub-zone Southern Wadden Sea. The four Wadden islands Vieland, Terschelling, Ameland and Schiermoonigkoog delimit the area from the offshore sea. Therefore, the region defined for this research under the name "Frisian Wadden Sea" is composed of the land along the coastline of the Dutch province Friesland starting with the Afsluitdijk in the South and ending at the Lauwersmeer in the North while stretching up to 10 km inland. Furthermore, the four Wadden islands named above are also included in the defined area. Figure 1 illustrates the designated destination Frisian Wadden Sea.

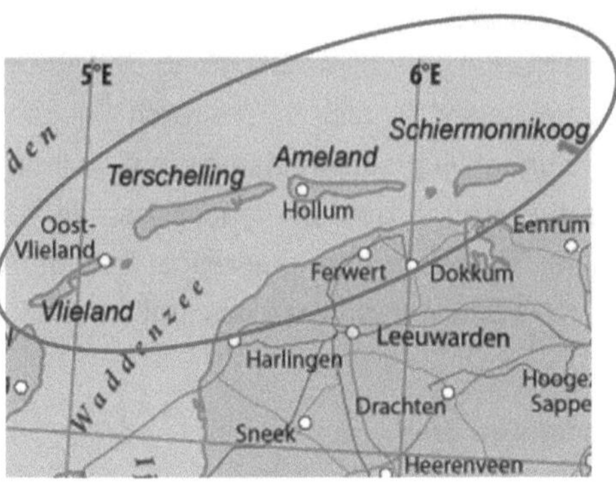

Figure 1 The Frisian Wadden Sea area (Source: MapXL, 2012)

There are no major cities in this zone, the biggest municipality being Franekeradeel with 20,501 inhabitants in 2012 (CBS 2012). The city of Leeuwarden which is the capital of Friesland and has a population of 95,321 people is located approx. 25 km from the coast (CBS 2012). The highest elevation is 25 m above N on Vieland, yet the average altitude of the area is 2 m below N (CWSS 2008). This is due to the fact that most of the land consists of so called *Polders*, that is drenched land which has been secured by dykes along the coastline (CWSS 2008). The climate is strongly influenced by the sea and has a temperate maritime character with relatively mild winters and rather cool summers. The average temperature in July is 16.5 °C, while the mean temperature in January is 2.5 °C. However, the annual perception averages 826 mm and can be mainly attributed to the strong western or north-western winds that bring in humid air masses from the Atlantic Ocean (CWSS 2008; Koniklijk Nederlands Meteorologisch Instituut n.a.). The tides have a rhythm of approx. six hours, thus the tidal flats fall dry and flood twice a day. The landscape has also been shaped by the sea, due to continuous influence from floods and sedimentation. Dominating features are coastal wetlands composed of tidal flats, salt marshes, beaches, dunes and shoals. The West Frisian Islands are dune islands and built a natural barrier that protects the mainland coast from high waves of the offshore waters. Yet, the water between the islands and the main coast is very shallow, only reaching 15 m depth at its deepest point.

Due to the dynamic nature of the landscape, the flora and fauna that has emerged in this habit is at the same time specific and diverse. A rich variety of different plants and flowers can be found on the tidal marshes such as the European beach grass which blossoms on the sand dunes of the region. The waters from the offshore bring in an abundance of microorganisms with every high tide that serve as a food basis for the worms, shellfish, sand hoppers and mussels which live in the tidal flats. The relatively warm waters of the shallow Wadden Sea are used as a breeding ground by many fish species from the open sea, such as sole, plaice and dab. Due to the high availability of nutrition the Wadden Sea is also home to a multitude of bird species. Moreover, the area constitutes an important resting place for many migrant birds on their journey to or from Africa. Lastly, the Frisian Wadden Sea is home to about 8,000 grey seals and harbor seals and thereby the most important habitat for grey seals in the entire Wadden Sea. Overall, the Wadden Sea forms a worldwide unique eco-system that is created by the interplay of various environmental factors. This was the determining reason for its nomination of as *UNESCO* world-heritage in 2009 (CWSS 2008; CWSS n.a.). Historically the area of Dutch Friesland was first settled around 500 BC. These early settlers built their villages on self-constructed earthen hills, so called *Terpen* to protect them from flooding. As technology advanced, dykes were developed which allowed the Frisian population to separate land from the sea, which was subsequently drenched and used as new settlement and farming area. The first cities developed in the 10th and 11th century the oldest ones being Stavoren and Leeuwarden (Mostert 2001; CWSS 2008).

3.2 Destination image

It has been stated that people have mental pictures or opinions about a place, even though they might have never actually visited it (Gunn 1988). In tourism literature this phenomenon is known as destination image and it has been a frequently studied subject in tourism research over the last three decades (Tasci, Gartner et al. 2007). However, as described in the next paragraph, there are different approaches towards the concept.

3.2.1 Components of destination images

When revising academic literature about destination image theory, two structural models describing destination image components become apparent, both of which have been used as a basis for image research and measurement (Echtner and Ritchie 1993; Gallarza, Saura et al. 2002).

The first model identifies three main elements of destination images. Its validity has been empirically verified by Baloglu and McCleary (1999). According to this concept, a destination image is composed of both cognitive and affective factors that together will form an overall notion about the destination, also known as global image. Cognitive image attributes include all aspects of information held about the destination which are reflected in the mind of a person as knowledge or opinions. As opposite to these, affective image traits result in an emotional evaluation of a destination by appealing to one´s feelings (Baloglu and Brinberg 1997; Baloglu and McCleary 1999). The three components and their relationships are illustrated in figure 2.

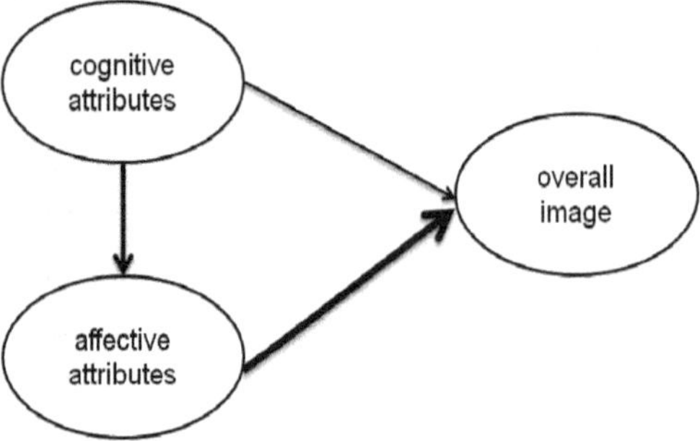

Figure 2 Components of destination image (according to Baloglu and McCleary 1999)

Drawing from the results of their research Baloglu and McCleary (1999) conclude that before visitation of the destination, the cognitive image is influenced by the type and range of information sources, consulted, with word-of-mouth being the agent that impacts most. Moreover, the socio-demographic characteristics, age and education also contribute to the cognitive evaluation. The affective image is largely based on the cognitive impressions of the destination. However, the variety and type of information as well as one´s individual travel motivations such as knowledge, prestige, social reasons and excitement also bias the emotions related to the destination. Although both cognitive and affective image build the global image, the latter was found to have a higher impact. Since this component is manipulated by cognitive impressions, it can be said that the affective evaluation of the destination serves as an intermediate between cognitive and overall image (Baloglu and McCleary 1999).

A similar study examining factors influencing the destination image of actual tourists, those being divided into first-time visitors and repeaters, was conducted by Beerli and Martín (Beerli and Martín 2004). The authors came to the conclusion that out of different types of information sources, mass media and particularly guide books execute the heaviest impact on cognitive image evaluation. Word-of-mouth was found to be the most credible and honest information agent, while advertisement, with the exception of travel agency staff, did not have a significant effect on the cognitive image. Furthermore, the number of excursions to attractions, undertaken during the stay, shapes the cognitive impressions of the destination´s natural and cultural attributes among first-timers. In other words, the more tourists engage in active sight-seeing at the destination, the more positive they will perceive natural and cultural features of the place. In addition, an individual´s overall travel experience contributes to the cognitive image of first-timers, yet to the affective image of repeaters. Congruent with Baloglu and McClearys´ findings, travel motivations proved to be correlated to the affective component. Consequently, the emotional evaluation was more positive if the motivations were met with according offers by the destination. Lastly, out of various socio-demographic variables, the country of origin is a crucial factor in the formation of both, cognitive and affective destination image (Beerli and Martín 2004).

In conclusion, the described model provides an overview over the different components that compose the construct destination image and identifies the relationships and hierarchies between them. In addition, various factors influencing the image elements have been recognized and this knowledge has important implications when efforts to manipulate the destination image are made (Beerli and Martín 2004). Moreover, the model has been reflected in destination branding literature, where the components describe different types of brand associations (Cai 2002; Qu, Kim et al. 2011). For this reason, the models components were included in the image assessment in the empirical part of this research.

Another approach to destination image is a three-dimensional concept introduced by Echtner and Ritchie (2003), which is based on three different continuum axes that describe six image components. In the first place, they differentiate between individual image attributes and a holistic image that encompasses all impressions held about a destination. The individual attributes stand for specific characteristics of a destination such as the climate, the landscape etc. These traits can be either of functional or psychological nature. Hence, they form the second continuum scale in Echtner and Ritchie´s model. Functional attributes are rational characteristics, thus they can be captured with measurement or observation techniques. Examples are the availability of tourists` sights, the standard of accommodation or the quality of shopping facilities. In contrast, psychological attributes are more difficult to assess since they relate to more emotional or subjective qualities, i.e. the friendliness of residents or the atmosphere of a place (Echtner and Ritchie 1993; Echtner and Ritchie 2003). Moreover, the third dimension stands for the difference between unique image factors in comparison to those that can be found throughout all destinations. Unique components are attributes that are specific to a given destination and can therefore serve to distinguish a destination (Echtner and Ritchie 2003; Keller 2003). Oppositely, common traits are features which are universal and can be measured in any destination as for instance price levels or quality of service. Naturally, both unique and common characteristics can be functional or psychological in nature. Furthermore, not all features of a destination image fit exclusively into one dimension since these are interrelated and should not be contemplated as separately, but rather as different aspects of the same subject (Echtner and Ritchie 1993; Echtner and Ritchie 2003). By differentiating between single attributes and the overall impression of a place as well as unique and common features and their functional or psychological quality a detailed, yet rather complex model examining various layers of image has been created. Out of these components, particularly the unique attributes were included in the research in order to identify characteristic traits and possible points of differentiation for the destination. Figure 3 visualises the outlined components, however, one has to keep in mind that this concept needs to be pictured three-dimensional.

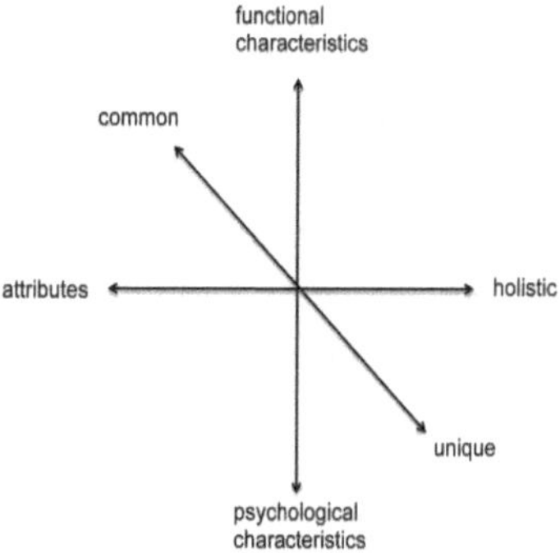

Figure 3 Components of destination image after Echtner and Ritchie (Source: Echtner and Ritchie 2003, p. 43)

Both models describe destination image with the help of various components and this knowledge is necessary in order to understand the concept's nature and define it.

3.2.2 Terminology and nature of construct

The term destination image regularly appears throughout tourism literature, yet there is no commonly agreed definition of the concept. Furthermore, many available definitions are imprecise and do not provide an integral view on the construct (Echtner and Ritchie 2003; Beerli and Martín 2004; Tasci, Gartner et al. 2007). One of the earliest definitions was made by Hunt (1975, p. 1) who referred to destination image as "perceptions held by potential visitors about an area". As one can see, this definition focuses only on potential visitors, although actual tourists and even residents also possess images of destinations (Gallarza, Saura et al. 2002; Beerli and Martín 2004). Moreover, it only highlights the cognitive component of an image, while no mention is made of affective or overall image. The latter appears in Crompton's study of the destination image of Mexico (1979, p.18) which states that "an image may be defined as the sum of beliefs, ideas and impressions that a person has of a destination". However, it does not account for the affective elements of destination image. Another approach has been taken by Gartner (1989, p.16) who delineates the term as "a complex combination of various products and associated attributes". Hence, he emphasizes the supply chain oriented nature of the tourism product, yet also disregards the affective component of destination images. Finally, a terminology that encompasses the cognitive, affective and global aspects of destination image has been given by Kim and Richardson (2003, p.218) who conceptualized it as "a totality of impressions, beliefs, ideas, expectations and feelings accumulated towards a place over time". Since the construct destination image is assessed under the focus of these components in this study, this definition shall be applied throughout it.

Having defined the term, it is necessary to closer examine the nature of the construct in order to gain a better understanding of dimensions and challenges involved in this research. Gallarza et al. (2002) have developed a conceptual framework in which they describe four attributes of destination images, the first of these being complexity. Destination images are complex because they can carry diverse meanings due to a lack of a universally accepted definition or approach towards the concept. In addition to the many existing definitions, different models describing various components have been established and varying opinions on nature, elements and methodical approaches towards measurement further contribute to the complexity of the issue. Secondly, destination images have a multiple nature. This is due to the dualism between attribute-based and global image. Furthermore, the formation of the destination image itself is influenced by numerous factors and constitutes a process that is composed of several stages. Yet another characteristic of destination images is relativism. Every individual forms his or her own image of a destination, hence images are subjective. In addition, the images of different destinations can be compared to each other, which makes them relative in reflection to their competitors. Finally, the nature of destination images is dynamic. This implies that they change according to the variables time and space. The former can be explained with the formation process which, in the course of various phases, leads to the alteration of images. When looking at the influence of space it can be seen that geographical location is an important factor in image formation (Beerli and

Martín 2004). It has been established that destination images become more realistic and detailed with shorter distance to the place (Fakeye and Crompton 1991).

The described characteristics of destination images form an important part in the conceptualization of the construct and constitute the basis for understanding image formation and choosing adequate measurement methods. Thus, they also have practical implications for research on the topic (Gallarza, Saura et al. 2002).

3.2.3 The image formation process

As previously pointed out, the formation of destination images is influenced by various factors such as sources of information, motivations and socio-demographic characteristics. However, with respect to its dynamic nature, it can also be regarded as a process, altering over time while passing through several stages (Gallarza, Saura et al. 2002). Gunn (1988) claims that a person can hold an image of a destination even though he or she has never been to the location and might not even be consciously considering visiting it or seeking for related information. Therefore, a major differentiation has to be made between the images of persons who have never actually visited the destination and form their image on the basis of secondary information in opposite to those that have been to the destination and therefore dispose of first-hand experience (Fakeye and Crompton 1991). Phelps (1986) classifies these types of images as secondary and primary image, with the former referring to potential and the later to actual tourists. However, particularly the secondary image can be further sub-divided into two phases during which the pre-visit images follow an evolution due to different types of information consulted. Firstly, an organic or informal image is produced as an outcome of information about a destination that does not carry a selling intention, but is merely informative (Gunn 1988; Fakeye and Crompton 1991; Mansfeld 1992). Examples for such sources of information are the mass-media or word-of-mouth (Echtner and Ritchie 2003). In this context a nation´s general image has to be considered, since it has been found to affect destination images (UNWTO 1980). Only once an individual starts to deliberately reflect commercial information about the destination, the next phase of image formation commences and the induced or formal image is established. During this stage, messages such as advertisement elaborated by the tourism industry which aim at promoting and selling a destination are the main types of information influencing the image formation (Gunn 1988; Fakeye and Crompton 1991; Mansfeld 1992). When potential tourists take the decision to undertake a journey and in the following gather real experiences at the destination, the secondary induced image transforms into a primary image. Fakeye and Crompton (1991) have depicted this image type as complex, since it encompasses more details and differentiations than secondary images.

In summary, destination images are not static, but follow a process that is linked to travel decision making and the phases of travel experiences of the individual (Gunn 1988). Since valuable information for the planning of promotional strategies can be gained from the analysis of image differences, it is advisable to assess both secondary and primary destination images (Fakeye and Crompton 1991). Therefore, the destination image of the Frisian Wadden Sea was measured for potential and actual tourists in order to identify the images held in both stages.

3.2.4 Measurement

The empirical measurement of destination images is closely related to the complex and multiple nature of the construct as well as its formation process, since both components of images and phases of formation need to be considered for an assessment. Echtner and Ritchie (1993; 2003) have developed a framework for the measurement of destination images that was empirically verified in a study of four destinations. They argue that all image components identified by them need to be included in an assessment in order to gain a complete knowledge about the destination images held by tourists. Thus, measurement methods need to cover attribute-based and holistic image, both of them including functional and psychological aspects. Furthermore, the unique traits of a destination should be explored. This can be achieved by using a mixture of structured or unstructured techniques, with the former being more suitable to capture the attribute-based image, i.e. with the help of attribute ratings on Likert-Scales. However, unique and holistic image components cannot be investigated by providing pre-determined content. In contrast, the respondents should be encouraged to come up with individual associations themselves (Echtner and Ritchie 2003). Hence, three open questions that aim at capturing both holistic and unique image traits can be employed. The first one refers to the functional holistic image by asking "What images or characteristics come to mind when you think of xxx as a vacation destination" (Echtner and Ritchie 1993, p.5). The psychological holistic image can be measured with the question "How would you describe the atmosphere or mood that you would expect to experience while visiting xxx?"(Echtner and Ritchie 1993, p.5). Lastly, unique image elements can be identified by inquiring about characteristic and distinctive destination features. The analysis of these questions was done by first classifying the responses and subsequently calculating the frequency of the established categories (Echtner and Ritchie 1993).

Other researchers (Baloglu and McCleary 1999; Beerli and Martín 2004; San Martín and Rodríguez del Bosque 2008; Byon and Zhang 2010) have used the model of cognitive, affective and global image for measuring destination images. Cognitive elements are generally assessed in the same way Echtner and Ritchi suggested for the attribute-based image that is using a list of destination features and rating these with the help of scales. For instance Baloglu and McCleary (1999) used 15 different items to capture the cognitive image. The measurement of the affective image has first been addressed by Russell and Pratt (1980) who established four bipolar scales of adjectives that cover all possible emotions that compose an image. Moreover, the authors suggest that only two of these scales are needed to thoroughly explore the affective image, these being "pleasant- unpleasant" and "arousing-sleepy" or "gloomy-exciting" and "distressing-relaxing" (Russell and Pratt 1980, p.311). In their study of affective destination images Baloglu and Brinberg (1997) confirmed the validity of these scales and showed that they can also be applied to measure the affective images of macro destinations such as countries or regions. Finally, the global image manifests itself in a favourable or unfavourable total evaluation of the destination; hence it can be measured employing rating scales such as a Likert-Scale with labels ranging from "very positive" and "very negative" (Ahmed 1991; Baloglu and McCleary 1999, p. 879; Beerli and Martín 2004).

In conclusion, the measurement of destination images is rather complex due to the difficulties to assess all image components and thus gaining a complete overview. Therefore, a combination of structured and unstructured methods is most suitable to explore the construct. To gain an insight into unique as well as functional and psychological holistic components, the open questions suggested by Echtner and Ritchie (1993) were chosen as unstructured methods. Furthermore, Likert-Scales were used to assess the cognitive, affective and overall image traits since these have been proven as an effective and valid tool throughout a large number of destination image studies (Ahmed 1991; Echtner and Ritchie 1993; Baloglu and Brinberg 1997; Baloglu and McCleary 1999; Beerli and Martín 2004; Pike 2009)

Naturally, the results of destination image analysis allow for conclusions about the destination´s attractiveness to target markets. This relationship is discussed in the next paragraph.

3.2.5 Destination image and choice of destination

Since even persons that have never visited a destination have a mental image of it, the decision to visit a destination and therefore choosing for it above other options is partly based on the notions and perceptions about the place (Gunn 1988; Um and Crompton 1990; Tasci, Gartner et al. 2007). During the holiday decision process, an organic destination image is usually transformed into an induced image due to the more commercial character of information sources that are being consulted in this phase (Fakeye and Crompton 1991). At the same time, the attractiveness of a destination is evaluated and crucially influences the destination selection, since only appealing options are considered for visiting. As noted by Hu and Ritchie (1993), destination attractiveness is built on both external and internal aspects. Internal factors refer to an individual's motivations and personal characteristics, whereas external input is heavily influenced by the destination image. Moreover, it has been found that the affective image has more impact on destination attractiveness than the cognitive image component. However, with increasing experience and expertise, cognitive aspects seem to gain more importance for attractiveness (Kim and Perdue 2011). Thus, destinations with a positive image are more likely to be visited since they are considered more attractive and therefore more apt to fulfill the demands for a satisfying holiday (Fakeye and Crompton 1991; Baloglu and McCleary 1999; Tasci, Gartner et al. 2007). Once the holiday has been completed and a complex destination image has been formed, this image also influences the tourist's behavioural intentions regarding repeated visitation and recommendation to others (Chen and Tsai 2007). Consequently, in the empirical part of this research behavioural intentions were measured in the form of likelihood to visit in order to investigate its relationship to destination image and thus draw conclusions about the destination's attractiveness.

Since image has been found to be decisive factor in destination selection, the importance of destination images for the success of tourism development can be claimed to be high (Hunt 1975). Therefore, destinations should carefully monitor and evaluate the image they project and that is held by their target markets (Tasci and Gartner 2007). In addition to considering the destination image, branding strategies can be employed to further increase destination attractiveness and likelihood of visiting (UNWTO 2009).

3.3 Destination branding

In the present tourism market, tourists can choose from an extensive range of places to visit all over the world. As a result, destinations face fierce competition. In response, the concept of destination branding has been introduced as an effective marketing tool (UNWTO 2009). It originates from the consumer product and service industry where branding has long been recognised as a mean to create a long-term competitive advantage (Aaker 1991; Keller 2003). Furthermore, branding of destinations has been proven to be an instrument capable of altering destination images by creating desirable associations (UNWTO 2009).

3.3.1 The nature of destination brands

The *UNWTO* (2009, p.xxx) has defined destination branding as "a summation of a destination´s or place´s characteristics that make it different and distinctive in the eyes of its potential visitors [...]. This gives it a competitive edge, which makes it stand out from its competitors." As can be seen from this definition a brand is more than symbol, logo or slogan, yet it is equal with the destination´s competitive identity since it comprises the unique and outstanding features of a place. Moreover, the brand embodies the fundamental nature of the destination (UNWTO 2009). This is congruent with Cai´s (2002, p.734) definition of destination branding "to select a consistent mix of brand elements to identify and distinguish a destination through positive image building". Therefore, a brand can be considered as the link between destination resources and the visitors or potential visitors´ awareness and perception of them. Since this last definition brings branding in the context of destination images, it shall be used as a basis for this research. In conclusion, destination branding can be regarded as the foundation of competitiveness for the destination and therefore it should be central to all communications and marketing programmes as well as to stakeholder behaviour (UNWTO 2009).

However, due to the complex nature of destinations, the branding of these poses unique challenges. Destinations are complex because they neither manufacture nor own the product they promote. Thus, they have limited control over its structure and quality. Furthermore, due to the supply chain oriented nature of the tourism product, many factors and parties influence the final product, adding to the difficulties of achieving a standardized product. Most core assets are part of the natural and cultural heritage of the destination and branding needs to be based on this given resources (UNWTO 2009). Thus, the specialties of destination branding lie in the challenge to present the reality at the destination while promoting it attractively. Moreover, the role of residents is particularly important for destination branding, since they ultimately form part of the visitor experience. Therefore, they need to understand and approve of the brand values in order to transmit them to tourists. Particularly during the development of the brand identity residents need to be involved in the identification of core values and brand elements (UNWTO 2009). Hence, the brand associations and brand identity that were developed as an outcome of this research and are based on the image held by the source market need to be evaluated and complemented by the region's residents.

There are two types of destination brands, namely geographic or thematic ones. Geographic brands strictly refer to a certain geographic area, such as cities, regions or nations, which is why they usually bear the name of the branded area. In contrast, thematic branding focuses on particular topics such as wellness, wine or water-sports. By doing so, they appeal to specific market segments. A destination may launch several brands as long as they all communicate the same brand identity, hence carrying the same core values. Thus, geographic or thematic branding can be used complementary (UNWTO 2009). Since the focus of this research is on the development of a brand identity, either a geographic or thematic brand can be built on this identity in a later stage of the branding process.

3.3.2 Functions and advantages of branding

Just as branding of products or services, destination branding is implemented in order to achieve several objectives. Destination brands serve to differentiate the destination from competitors, enhance knowledge of the destination due to higher awareness, inducing a favourable image and to establish a strong identity (UNWTO 2009). If these aims are achieved they create a number of advantages for both consumer and organisation. Familiar brands imply a unique meaning for consumers, because they promise a certain level of quality and have well-known characteristics. Therefore, they act as a risk reducer and facilitate the buying decision process, because the consumer is more confident to take a choice. Furthermore, search for information becomes more rapid due to increased efficiency and reduced need for interpretation. Hence, search time and costs decrease. If a consumer already knows what to expect from a brand, its use will result in higher satisfaction and subsequently is more likely to be repeated. Some users identify with brands and regard them as a reflection of their lifestyle and values, which creates particularly strong bonds with the brand (Aaker 1991; Keller 2003). For organisations, branding acts as a mean to enrich a product with unique features and thus gain a competitive advantage. Moreover, it enables the organisation to project a signal of quality and to augment user identification which impact consumer behaviour and support brand loyalty. Overall, branding results in more efficient marketing and higher profits for organisations (Aaker 1991; Keller 2003).

3.3.3 Brand equity, brand identity and brand associations

As previously discussed, strong brands bring benefits to consumers and organizations. When combined, these advantages describe the actual value of a brand. This concept is also known as brand equity (Aaker 1991; Keller 2003). Aaker (1991) identified five categories of brand assets that together create value and therefore form brand equity, namely brand loyalty, brand awareness, perceived quality, brand associations and other assets. Out of these groups, brand associations account for the divers mental linkages consumers relate to the brand. A similar approach towards brand equity has been taken by Keller (2003), who argues that the value of a brand is based on brand knowledge. This consumer knowledge of the brand can be divided into brand awareness and brand image. While brand awareness refers to recognition and degree of consciousness of the brand, the brand image has been defined as "perceptions about a brand as reflected by the brand associations held in consumer memory" (Keller 2003, p. 66). Hence, both authors agree that mental associations which consumers link to the brand are crucial components of brand equity. The main source for these associations is the brand identity, which evokes and sustains them in the consumers' minds by alluding to the core elements of the brand (Aaker 1996). Consequently, Aaker (1996, p. 68) defines brand identity as "a unique set of brand associations that the brand strategist aspires to create or maintain. These associations represent what the brand stands for and imply a promise to customers from the organization members". Hence, the brand identity can be regarded as the essence of a brand, because it yields the very values that a brand encompasses. Subsequently, it serves as a guideline for the organisation by giving "direction, purpose and meaning" (Aaker 1996, p. 68). Furthermore, it is the basis for the brand image and brand position. In this context, Aaker (1996) describes four misconceptions about brand identity, which help to distinguish these interrelated concepts. Firstly, the brand image as previously explained reflects the consumers' perceptions of a brand. However, while brand identity should be built on these associations it does not equal the brand image. During the development phase of the brand identity, the image constitutes a valuable source of information for the identities' core elements and values. In continuation, once the identity has been established and grown strong, it can influence and change the consumers' brand image. The second identity trap refers to brand positioning. This includes all communications that aim to situate the brand in the minds of the target group members. Brand positioning should comprise selected elements of the brand identity, yet some identity components might not be intended for external publication, but rather for the organisation itself. Both brand image and brand positioning consider the external perspective of a brand; however, the brand identity also possesses an internal side. Organisation members, in the case of destinations being residents and tourism suppliers, have an important role in the brand's identity. They need to understand and accept its core values in order to represent it to the public. Therefore, the brand identity must not be solely formed on the basis of external orientation, but also carefully consider internal knowledge, opinions and concerns. The last misconception about brand identity deals with the nature of brand associations. Too often, these are based entirely on product or service attributes, while non-functional features such as intangible perceptions are neglected. Yet, a brand is more than a product or service itself and its identity must inspire associations that imply a range of functional, emotional and self-expressive user benefits (Aaker 1996). Furthermore, Aaker suggests that there are different types of brand associations.

These have been further illustrated by Keller (2003) who distinguishes between attributes, benefits and attitude perceptions of a brand. Attributes refer to brand characteristics, such as functional features. Hence, this category involves all associations that are related to the brand's performance. Perceptions about benefits are founded in the evaluation of intangible and emotional brand features, such as use occasion or personal values. Thus, brand benefits are notions of advantages gained from the consumption of the brand. They depend to a large extend on the psychographic traits of the consumer. The third class of associations are brand attitudes, which account for the general rating of the brand and essentially determine consumer behaviour (Keller 2003). Moreover, all perceptions of a brand inspired by the brand identity should be strong, favourable and unique in nature. This is due to the fact that only brand associations which are sufficiently relevant, positive and distinguish the brand from competitors will contribute to the formation of an affirmative brand image and hence support brand equity (Keller 2003).

3.3.4 The branding process

Building a strong brand and consequently attaining brand equity is the final goal of the branding process. At the beginning of this process stands the creation and establishment of the brand. In order to achieve this, certain steps need to be followed and attention should be paid to consumers´ and other stakeholders´ needs at all times (Keller 2003; UNWTO 2009). For the development of a new brand, four steps have been identified that build upon each other and conclude in customer-based brand equity in the form of loyalty and attachment to the brand. The first stage is concerned with creating a brand identity. Hence; this phase determines the brand´s core elements and values. In continuation, the identity is enriched with a meaning that clarifies what the brand is about by allocating mental associations to the identity. In the third step positive brand responses are enhanced in order to establish a link between the brand and the consumer. In the last phase of brand building, the relationship between consumer and brand grows and results in interest, identification, attachment and loyalty (Keller 2003).

Since the first step deals with the creation of a brand identity, which has been found to be the essence of a brand, its development involves several considerations and sub-phases, which can be described with the help of various models, such as the six-level brand pyramid or the brand wheel (UNWTO 2009). With the brand wheel, the facts and symbols of a brand, as well as its values, personality, benefits, proposition and essence are illustrated in concentric layers. While the brand essence constitutes the core element of the wheel, brand personality and proposition form the second layer. The proposition thereby refers to those brand qualities that make it unique and grant a competitive advantage. The ultimate coating of the wheel is composed of facts and symbols of the brand as well as its values. On the one hand, brand personality and values relate to emotional aspects of the brand, whereas on the other hand brand proposition and facts and symbols are concerned with the rational facet. Furthermore, in addition to the brand elements, the model encompasses a consideration of the destination as touristic product and its consequences from both a rational and affective perspective (UNWTO 2009). This makes it more detailed than the brand pyramid, yet the various components do not build upon each other as in the pyramid.

The six level brand pyramid uses brand attributes as initial point for the brand identity development and over the course of six stages educes the brand essence (see figure 4).

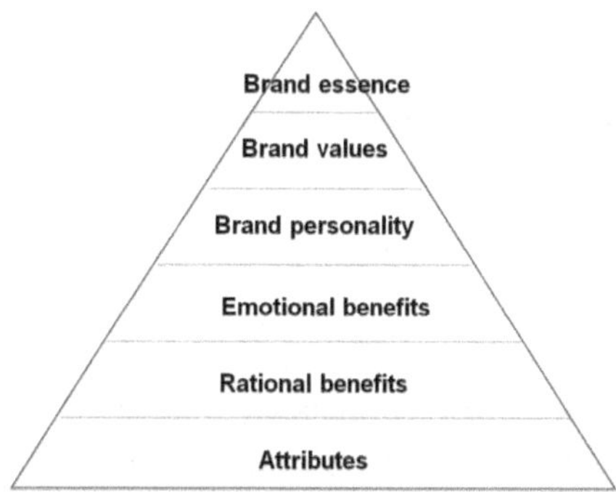

Figure 4 Six-stage brand pyramid (Source, UNWTO 2009, p. 47)

The first stage refers to destination features and characteristics. These constitute the basis for the brand identity, because they compose the reality at the destination. The attribute stage is followed by rational benefits which relate to functional and tangible advantages drawn from the destination features. For instance, this might include easy accessibility or inexpensiveness. Furthermore, consumers or as in the case of destinations tourists attach feelings to a destination and seek emotional benefits from their visit. Knowledge of this type of benefits is important for identity development, because they reveal which psychological motivations the destination can and should satisfy. The two classes of benefits are the foundation for the brand personality. At this stage, unique characteristics of the destination are identified. Its purpose in the brand identity building process is to embody all key associations that should be evoked in the hearts and minds of actual and potential visitors by appealing to their rational and emotional needs. Drawing from the brand personality, the core brand values can be identified. These are values and attitudes that the destination stands for. To conclude the identity creation, the very essence of the brand is defined on the sixth and last level of the pyramid. It consists of three to four core elements that form the enduring and fundamental nature of the brand. Together, brand values and essence make up the crucial aspects of the brand identity (UNWTO 2009).

Even though the brand wheel is more comprehensive with regards to destination marketing strategy, the six stage pyramid was chosen as basis for this research because in this model functional attributes and emotional evaluations constitute the foundation for determining the brand values and essences. Therefore, it reflects the destination image and builds the brand identity on the perceptions held about the destination, which is congruent with the aim of this research.

However, once the identity has been developed and the brand has been established in the market, the strategic brand management process which aims to achieve long-term brand equity has not been completed yet. The brand performance needs to be constantly monitored and analysed, e.g. in the form of brand audits. Finally, the growth and sustainability of brand equity have to be ensured by implementing brand expansion strategies such as enhancing brand equity over various market segments (Keller 2003).

3.3.5 Branding and destination image

Having discussed the nature and development process of destination brands, the relationship to the destination image construct shall be explored. Both concepts are closely related, because they build on each other (Cai 2002; Qu, Kim et al. 2011). Although a brand is more than an image, because it yields the destination´s competitive identity, its success is partly attributable to the destination image (Tasci and Kozak 2006). The linkage between the two constructs consists in the brand identity, which essentially reflects the key associations of the destination. These associations are a synonym for the image components of destination images. While cognitive image evaluations are mirrored in attribute based brand associations, the affective image elements can be found in the notions about benefits gained from the brand. Brand attitudes consist of an overall evaluation of the destination and hence equal the global image. Furthermore, they form the foundation for visitor behaviour (Cai 2002; Pike 2009). In addition, the unique image components described by Echtner and Ritchie (2003) are crucial for determining unique brand associations that help to differentiate the destination and compose the brand personality (Cai 2002; Qu, Kim et al. 2011). Since the brand identity draws its power from the related associations, it will only be strong and meaningful if these associations match the image components and are accepted by the target audience. This is why during the brand identity building, the destination image held by potential and actual visitors needs to be carefully considered (Cai 2002; UNWTO 2009). These valuable insights into the destination image of the target group can be gained with the help of market research, which should be conducted prior to all branding activities (Morgan 2002; UNWTO 2009). Once the brand identity has been established, it can influence the destination image by projecting a positive brand image. Hence, a differentiation needs to be made between the terms destination image and brand image. While the former refers to the perceived image by visitors, the latter describes the image projected by the destination marketing organisation. Ideally the image perceived by the target group should be identical with the projected image. When monitoring branding efforts, the gap between these two sides of an image should be assessed and in continuation, measurements to overcome these misperceptions have to be taken (Tasci and Kozak 2006; Qu, Kim et al. 2011).

3.3.6 Brand positioning

Since the global destination market is highly competitive due to the abundance of travel destinations, branding has become an important mean for gaining a competitive advantage and thus increasing visitor numbers (Morgan, Pritchard et al. 2004). In order to achieve such an advantage, the brand needs to successfully differentiate itself from competitors. This is done by brand positioning. It deals with the creation of points of differences in the target markets perception of the destination (Lovelock and Wirtz 2004). Hence, once a destination has identified the market segment with most potential, it needs to consider how to position itself in the most appealing way to this target group (Kotler and Armstrong 2004). Congruently, Kotler (2003, p.202) argues that positioning is "the act of designing the company´s offering and image to occupy a distinctive place in the target markets minds". By applying this concept to destinations, Crompton (1992, p.20) defines the positioning of destinations as "the process of establishing and maintaining a distinctive place for a destination in the minds of potential visitors within the target markets". As drawing from these definitions positioning aims to establish the desired brand meaning and thus elicit a value proposition for the target group that will give it an incentive to choose for the destination. The brand identity constitutes the basis for the positioning efforts by providing the core brand associations and values as well as unique features. However, positioning takes the marketing of the brand one step further by evaluating the brand and its unique traits in reference to its competitors (Keller 2003; Kotler 2003; Kotler and Armstrong 2004). If implemented successfully, the target audience will accredit the destination an added value and this is likely to influence their perception of it (Ahmed 1991). However, in order to determine meaningful and valuable points of difference, knowledge of the customers´ preferences as well as an analysis of the competitors´ offerings is required. Therefore, Keller (2003) describes four steps to brand positioning, of which the first is to choose a promising target group through market segmentation. In continuation the main competitors are identified and the brand is assessed in relation to them. Knowledge about similarities and differences to these competing brands is gained as an outcome of this analysis from which points of difference can be determined. Therefore, developing a positioning strategy involves conducting three types of evaluations, namely market, internal and competitor analysis. The first of these provides insights to consumer preferences, perceptions and benefits sought. Internal evaluations refer to evaluation of the organisation´s resources and limitations for positioning. Lastly, the competitive analysis reveals the position of the brand in comparison to its competitors (Lovelock and Wirtz 2004). Once the main competitive advantages are identified as a result of these assessments, a positioning statement which phrases the overall positioning strategy in form of the positioning goal is elaborated (Kotler and Armstrong 2004). The positioning goal is identical with the desired position the destination strives to hold in the target market´s mind. Since positioning constitutes the foundation for the marketing action plan, it should be considered in all subsequently developed marketing strategies and hence impacts the entire marketing-mix. Thus, positioning the destination adequately can be regarded as the most crucial strategic marketing decision, since it essentially determines the destination´s attractiveness in the eyes of potential visitors and consequently affects their choice of destination (Aaker and Shansby 1982; Kotler and Armstrong 2004). Given that the positioning strategy is developed subsequently to the target group selection and aims to positively influence their behavioural intentions, it needs to be consequently orientated towards the customers´ needs, preferences and perceptions of the destination. Therefore, the destination image held by the target group is a key source of information for positioning. However, positioning is distinct from the image construct in the sense that it also considers competitive destinations and evaluates the destination image in relation to these. Once it has been effectively designed, the positioning strategy can be used to influence to destination image. In order to monitor the success of the selected positioning strategy, regular evaluations such as analysis of destination image and destination attractiveness in comparison to competing destinations, need to be conducted (Ahmed 1991; Crompton, Fakeye et al. 1992; Keller 2003; Pike 2009).

3.4 Conclusion

In conclusion, destination images crucially influence intentional behaviours and destination attractiveness and are therefore an important concept in tourism research and practice. Due to its complexity different components have been identified and various approaches for measurement have been suggested. Destination branding is a marketing strategy closely related to destination image and knowledge of the latter can be used as a source of information for the development of a brand identity. However, branding goes beyond image building since it aims to position the destination in the mind of the target group by differentiation from competitors. Since the Frisian Wadden Sea forms part of the wider Wadden Sea that stretches out over the Netherlands, Germany and Denmark, developing a unique brand identity is an important step towards positioning the destination on a competitive market. The theoretical background outlined in this chapter constitutes the basis for the investigation of the destination image of the Frisian Wadden Sea held by the German source market and provided the framework for the secondary analysis described in the next chapter.

4 Secondary research findings

In order to gain deeper knowledge of the image of the Frisian Wadden Sea and the research that had already been conducted on this topic, three Dutch studies, namely *Toerdata Noord Consumentenonderzoek 2009*, *Imago van de Waddeneilanden* and *Positie van Friesland op de Duitse vakantiemarkt* were examined. Firstly, the applied methodical approach and background information on data collection were considered. Relevant results were outlined, thus depicting the destination image of the analysed area. Moreover, the studies were analysed with regards to the destination image theory described in the literature review. Subsequently, the findings were considered with respect to primary research and questionnaire development.

4.1 Toerdata Noord Consumentenonderzoek 2009

The project *Toerdata Noord* from the *Stenden University of Applied Sciences* monitors the tourism supply and demand in the Northern Netherlands provinces Friesland, Groningen and Drenthe (ETFI 2012). Every four years, data about the tourism demand is collected from domestic and German tourists and published in the *Consumentenonderzoek* report. The latest study of this kind was conducted in 2009 and was carried out among a total of 3009 day-visitors and overnight-tourists (de Haas and Huig 2010). However, of these respondents, only approx. 2% were Germans, which is why the study mainly reflects a Dutch perspective. The three provinces have been divided into 12 regions, of which, when looking at the Frisian Wadden Sea, only the "Waddeneilanden" (Waddden islands) and "Overig Friesland" (rest of Friesland) are relevant (de Haas and Huig 2010, p.6). The data was collected on various days during the spring, summer and autumn season in the form of structured interviews following questions on a standardized questionnaire. As part of the research, the image of the regions was measured. This was done with the help of the open-ended question: "Wat vindt u het meest typerende van de provincie waar u zich nu, gedurende uw vakantie bevindt?" (de Haas and Huig 2010). This question can be translated as: "What do you find most typical for the province where you are now spending your holidays?" Hence, the respondents were to name spontaneous associations with the destination.

As judging from theory on destination image measurement, this method does not serve to gain an insight knowledge or comprehensive understanding of various components of the tourists' destination image (Echtner and Ritchie 1993; Baloglu and McCleary 1999). However, it gives an idea of the mental pictures that the tourists carry of the destination and its results provide an orientation for the development of the questionnaire. The following findings are taken from the results of the survey among overnight tourists that included 107 respondents in the Wadden islands region and 69 respondents in the rest of the Frisian region. The participants' answers were classified into nine categories that were used consistently in this survey. Table 1 lists these categories including a translation to English.

Original group labelling	Translated title
Actief (wandelen & fietsen)	Active (walking & biking)
Gezellig, vriendelijk en sfeervol	Homey, friendly and atmospheric
Overig	Others
Rust, Ruimte en natuur (flora & fauna)	Quietude, space and nature (flora& fauna)
Stad / dorp, winkelen / cultuur etc	Town/Village, Shopping/Culture etc.
Stug, saai, vlak, kaal, te rustig, ver weg	Austere, boring, flat, too quiet, far away
Tevredenheid (prima, goed, mooi etc)	Satisfaction (super, good, nice, etc.)
Veelzijdig en divers	Versatile and divers
Water (waterrijk, strand, meren, plassen, zwemmen, watersport (zeilen, varen))	Water (lots of water, beach, lakes, ponds, swimming, water sports (sailing))

Table 1 Image categories (According to: Consumentenonderzoek

In the region of the Wadden islands, perceptions fitting into the group *Quietude, space and nature* were mentioned most frequently, by 67% of the respondents. This was followed by *Homey, friendly and atmospheric* and *Water* with 10% and 9% respectively.

In the rest of Friesland region *Quietude, space and nature* was also the most common association, named by 43% of the respondents. However, 35% thought that water related aspects were the most typical for the region, while

9% stated impressions from the category *Town/Village, Shopping/Culture etc* in mind (Toerdata Noord 2010).

In summary, the respondents of the survey strongly associate natural aspects with the destination, particularly dominant being the presence of water. The tourists describe the destination as spacious and quiet, which paints the picture of an unhasty and relaxing atmosphere. Furthermore, it is perceived as cosy and friendly. Some of the tourists on the mainland also relate towns, culture and shopping to the destination, which can be explained by the fact that this region, unlike the Wadden islands, is not entirely restricted to the little urbanised coastline, but also includes towns like Leeuwarden.

Even though the overall image was not assessed, it can be assumed that the majority of the respondents held a positive holistic image, since predominantly favourable aspects were mentioned.

When applying destination image theory to this analysis, it can be found that the groups that were formed from the respondents' statements included both cognitive and affective components. The categories *Active, Town/village, shopping/culture*, *Water* and *Versatile and divers* describe cognitive functional attributes of the destination. *Homey, friendly and atmospheric* and *Satisfaction* relate to affective and psychological elements. Moreover, the groupings *Quietude, space and nature* as well as *Austere, boring, flat, too quiet, far away* combine both functional and emotional evaluations. Furthermore, neither unique features nor the overall image were included in the study. However, it has to be taken into account that this image analysis only formed part of a wider study and was not the main purpose of the research.

With regards to questionnaire development, the characteristics identified by the participants can be used as a guideline for the functional and affective attributes to be included in the questionnaire. Moreover, characteristic and specific attributes like unhasty or spacious could be used to measure unique image factors. Since the respondents were actual tourists who were familiar with the destination, the identified image attributes should be rather realistic (Fakeye and Crompton 1991).

4.2 Imago van de Waddeneiladen

The study *Imago van de Waddeneiladen* (Image of the Wadden islands) was conducted among a panel of the Dutch population between 16 and 65 years from the 8th until the 20th of December 2007. The survey was distributed online and a total of 1.038 questionnaires were evaluated. The aim of this study was to establish the image of the Wadden islands held by the Dutch population. A special emphasis was put on the comparison to other destinations within the Netherlands. Hence, the participants were asked to rank the attractiveness of the Wadden islands in relation to other Dutch destinations. Furthermore, the image of the Wadden islands in general was assessed by measuring the overall impression of the islands as a destination for short or long holidays on a 7-point Likert-Scale. In continuation a spontaneous statement on positive and negative characteristics of the islands was asked. Lastly, the respondents were presented a list with 20 types of vacations and activities which they had to rate in reference to suitability for the islands (de Rijk and Borger 2008).

The results of this study reveal that 83% of the participants have a positive attitude towards the Wadden islands as a holiday destination. In contrast, only 4% regarded the destination as negative. However, the general impression is more positive among visitors than among persons who have never been to the islands. When asked to name attractive characteristics of the destination, the most common answers were quietude, nature and associations related to the sea such as coast, beach or dunes with 43%, 39% and 34% respectively. Moreover, island feeling and space were named by 15% and 12% of the respondents. As negative aspects, a lack of events and activities (18%) and the dependency on ferries (15%) were mentioned. In addition, respectively 10% of the participants found the destination too far away and too busy or touristic. However, 27% of the respondents did not name any negative aspects about the destination (de Rijk and Borger 2008).

With regards to the rating of holiday types and activities, the islands were considered as a destination for nature experience and sustainability, relaxation and light physical activities like walking or biking by the majority of the participants as can be seen in figure 5. However, cultural activities (25%), visits to nightclubs (22%), shopping (18%) and visits to zoo (8%) scored rather low (de Rijk and Borger 2008).

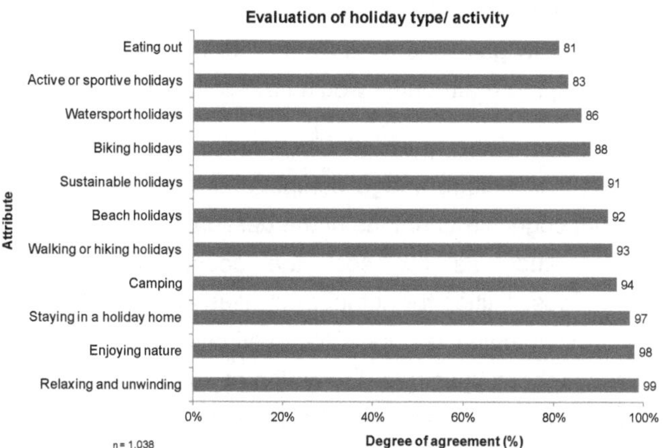

Figure 5 Evaluation of holiday type or activity (according to Imago van de Waddeneinlanden 2007)

To conclude, the destination image of the Wadden islands held by the Dutch population is that of a quiet, relaxing atmosphere with plenty of space. There are strong associations to the islands' natural assets, including attributes such as the sea, the coast, beaches or dunes. A rather unique component is the island feeling. Moreover, the islands seem to be positioned as a destination for outdoor activities like walking, biking and water-sports in the minds of the respondents. However, the participants also perceive the destination as far away and difficult to reach due to the dependency on ferry services. In addition, the majority has the notion that the offer of cultural and recreational activities is limited. Nonetheless, the overall destination image is positive for most participants. Furthermore, there is a difference between the images of potential and actual visitors, with actual visitors rating the destination more positive and describing it as more diverse.

With respect to destination image theory, the overall image, as well as cognitive and affective aspects was assessed with structured and unstructured questions. While the spontaneous associations reveal tangible and non-tangible characteristics of the destination, the list of holiday types and activities seems more suitable to describe the attractiveness of the destination for certain market segments rather than the destination image. Therefore, in order to gain deeper insights into this image by revealing its divers components, more attributes would have to be measured explicitly.

For the development of the questionnaire, conclusions about functional and emotional as well as unique image components can be drawn from these results. Important cognitive attributes of the destination image are the islands' natural features such as the sea, the coast, beaches and dunes. Furthermore, the possibilities for outdoor activities and sports state a tangible characteristic. Psychological factors of the destination image are described by the relaxing atmosphere, quietude, the notion of space and the island feeling on the Wadden islands. Particularly the latter is rather special and could therefore be used in a listing of unique image attributes.

4.3 Positie van Friesland op de Duitse vakantiemarkt

The comprehensive study *Positie van Friesland op de Duitse vakantiemarkt* was carried out by the *Nederlands bureau voor toerisme & congressen* (*NBTC*) on behalf of *Fryslân Marketing* and contains a chapter on the image of Friesland and the Dutch Wadden islands on the German market. The research was conducted with the assistance of the research agency *Blauw research* which used an online panel to collect answers from 1236 actual and potential visitors to Friesland and the Wadden islands in the period from the 6th until the 13th of December 2010. The respondents were between 18 and 65 years old. 397 participants had visited Friesland or the Wadden islands in the last two years, whereas further 839 respondents knew one of the two destinations, but had not been there yet. Firstly, the degree of awareness of the destinations was assessed with the help of a 5 point Likert- Scale. For the image analysis, the respondents were asked to spontaneously name aspects of the regions. Subsequently, they were provided with a list of 20 image attributes which they had to evaluate according to their suitability for the destination. Moreover, nine continuum scales with antithetic adjectives on both ends were tested for agreement in reference to the regions. An example of such a scale is the continuum open to closed (van der Most, Peters et al. 2011).

The findings presented in the report reveal that the Frisian Wadden islands are unknown to 26% of the respondents. Further 23% know the destination, but only by name, while another 20% are aware of it, but had never been there and 25% had already visited the islands for vacations. 6% had been to the region, but not for holidays. Interestingly, the participants of the border regions North Rhine-Westphalia and Lower Saxony show higher awareness of the destination than respondents from the rest of Germany. When asked for a spontaneous reaction on the Wadden islands, the terms mudflats, North Sea, beach and fresh air were expressed most commonly. Further popular namings were quietude, high or low tide, holiday, sea, mudflat hiking, nature and scenery. Overall, the majority of answers was related to the destination's natural features as well as to holiday activities (van der Most, Peters et al. 2011).

Likewise, in the evaluation of attributes, those that scored highest for the Wadden islands were related to the destination's nature and the atmosphere and recreational activities resulting from it. As can be seen in figure 6, the statement *Lovely landscape, beautiful scenery* achieved with 69% the highest degree of agreement among the participants. Furthermore, the respondents ascribed the islands as an unhasty environment with good possibilities for outdoor activities like biking and hiking as well as for holidays related to water. The residents are supposed to be friendly and welcoming. Congruent with the *Imago van de Waddeneiladen* study, the results for attributes related to shopping, accessibility, and opportunities for excursions and cultural activities were rather low. In addition, weather conditions and the availability of facilities for bad weather activities were perceived as low (van der Most, Peters et al. 2011).

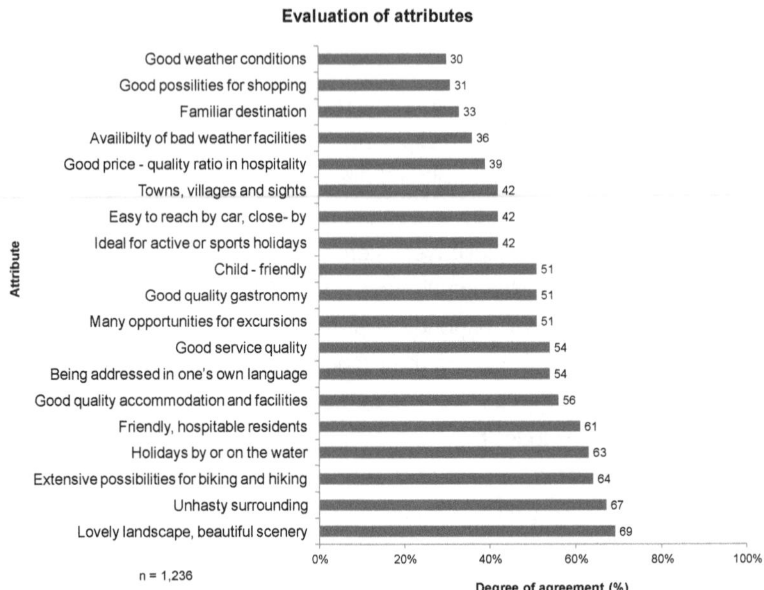

Figure 6 Evaluation of destination attributes (according to Positie van Friesland op de Duitse vakantiemarkt 2011)

Actual visitors assessed all attributes more positively than potential visitors. Particularly those attributes with low scores were rated higher by respondents that had already been to the region (van der Most, Peters et al. 2011). These results could indicate that there is a lack of information about the destination and its recreational offers in the market.

Drawing from the findings of the adjective continuum scales, the study's participants describe the Wadden islands as a green and natural destination. Furthermore, they regard the region as relatively interesting and diverse, however, with respect to these aspects, potential visitors perceive the destination as rather neutral for the scales boring vs. interesting and diverse vs. monotonous. Another rather neutral rating was given to the disparity between a frugal and a luxury destination with a slight inclination towards the former. There is general agreement that the islands are a safe region that has the ability to surprise its visitors while being inhabited by open and hospitable residents. Lastly, the respondents ascribe the islands a relaxed and unhasty atmosphere (van der Most, Peters et al. 2011).

To sum up the results of this research, the general destination image of the Dutch Wadden islands held by the German population can be described as that of a region with a quiet, relaxing atmosphere that is primarily known for its natural qualities. Hence, natural aspects, particularly those related to the North Sea, such as the mudflats, beaches, tides, wind or fresh air are the first characteristics that occurred to most persons when they thought of the destination and these attributes were also rated as most typically for the islands. As a result of this dominance of natural aspects, the region is regarded very positively in reference to outdoor activities or sports. The region's residents are considered as friendly and hospitable, thus adding to the positive image. In contrast, culture, sightseeing or other recreational activities such as shopping are not usually associated with the region. Furthermore, the weather conditions, price-quality ratio and accessibility are perceived as problematic. Another issue is the awareness of the region as a holiday destination, since almost one third of the respondents did not know the islands.

Congruently with the *Imago van de Waddeneiladen* study, differences between the images of actual and potential tourists could be identified. The images of those participants who had already visited the destination tended to be more positive and varied than those of persons who had not been to the islands.

Reflecting this study with regards to destination image theory, it becomes apparent that cognitive and psychological emotional image factors were measured. Yet, neither the overall image, nor unique image components were addressed. Nevertheless, useful information for the questionnaire development can be gained from the identified image components. For instance, functional elements named in the study are natural characteristics of the destination, such as the landscape, the sea and related features. Moreover, the suitability for recreational activities, such as mudflat hiking, walking, biking or excursions and the availability of quality hospitality, facilities and sights constitute functional aspects of the destination. Likewise do weather conditions, accessibility and child- friendliness. Psychological factors are represented in the attribute friendly residents. With regards to the list of adjectives, the affective image component was measured with the continuum boring-interesting which is similar to Russell´s (1981) sleepy-arousing scale. Furthermore, the scales with the extremes divers-monotonous, surprising-predictable and open-closed assess psychological attributes. The same applies for the scales frugal-luxury, relaxing-active and safe-unsafe. Only the continuum natural and green-urbanised represents a cognitive image factor.

A unique image component determined from this research could be the attribute unhasty surrounding.

4.4 Conclusion

In conclusion, this secondary research composed of three image analysis of the Frisian Wadden islands and coastline from the perspective of Dutch and German actual and potential visitors has shown that there are many parallels in the image traits described in these three studies. However, it has to be taken into account that the image measurement methods were rather similar, since mainly functional and psychological emotional attributes were assessed, while insufficient attention was paid to holistic and unique image factors. Therefore, better insights on this last component shall be gained from primary research by investigating possible unique factors identified from the results of the analysed studies.

The image depicted from this analysis is that throughout these studies, the Frisian Wadden Sea area is commonly perceived as a destination with a quiet, relaxing atmosphere due to an unhasty environment. Furthermore, the local residents are considered friendly and welcoming. The respondents of the *Toerdata Noord* study also ascribed the region certain cosiness. However, since this survey was carried out mainly among Dutch participants it has to be investigated whether Germans have a similar notion about this attribute.

Moreover, the destination's nature seems to be well positioned in the minds of both Dutch and German visitors, since all attributes related to this feature received high ratings and also appeared as primary namings in spontaneous statements throughout all analysed studies. Particularly those natural assets related to the water and the coastline such as the sea, beaches, dunes, wind and fresh air were pointed out. Although being one of the most unique characteristics of the destination, the mudflats and related activities were only mentioned by the participants of one study. All surveys agree that the destination is well suited for outdoor activities such as walking, biking or mudflat hiking. Yet, there is general consent that the destination does not offer a great variety of cultural activities or recreational entertainment such as shopping.

Drawing from these findings, the following unique image components could be determined: Firstly, the mudflats of the Frisian Wadden Sea area constitute a rare natural characteristic which also offers opportunities for related activities such as mudflat hiking. Secondly, probably due to the low degree of urbanisation, the destination is perceived as spacious and vast which could also differentiate the region from competing destinations if primary research confirms the uniqueness of this attribute. Moreover, this is likely to contribute to the unhasty and relaxing atmosphere that was depicted by the majority of participants of the analysed surveys. Combined with the attribute cosiness, this specific type of island feeling could be characteristic for the destination.

Based on the results from secondary analysis, empirical research was conducted to measure consistency with these findings as well as to deepen the knowledge and understanding of the image among German visitors.

5 Methodology

The primary research for the image analysis of the Frisian Wadden Sea was conducted in the form of an empirical, descriptive study using non-experimental methods (Veal 1997; Saunders, Lewis et al. 2007). The findings from the desk-research constituted the basis for the primary data collection. The latter encompassed quantitative methods in the form of a survey which further explored the destination image of the Frisian Wadden Sea held by actual and potential German visitors. The survey population was therefore the entire German population aging 18 years and older.

5.1 Survey method

The survey method encompassed both an online survey as well as self-administered questionnaires in printed format. The online survey was created on the platform *google docs* and the link to the online questionnaire was distributed via chain e-mailing as well as placed on two blogs about the Netherlands and four online travel forums (see appendix 1). The printed forms were distributed on the island Ameland in the Frisian Wadden Sea area on two different days of the week and different times of the day. In addition, questionnaires were given out to six hotels of different size and categories on the same island with the petition to distribute them among German guests.

Since online and printed questionnaires were used for data collection, hence employing more than one method, this research constitutes a mixed-mode survey. In this case, the issue of data integrity is particularly relevant and needs to be evaluated in the research design. Even though there are different mixed-mode approaches, for this project only the type "different modes for different respondents" is of concern, since data is collected both in the form of an online questionnaire and with the help of a self- administered paper questionnaire (De Leeuw and Hox 2011, p.51). The premise is that different modes might cause different responses, hence threatening data reliability. However, various studies which have been summarised by de Leeuw and Hox (2011) have established that in the case of mixed-mode design using online and printed self-administered questionnaires with the same set of questions, data equivalency can be assumed. Thus, the quality of results was not reduced by the employment of the mixed-mode method.

5.2 Questionnaire development

The survey questionnaire was developed with the knowledge that had been acquired from literature review and secondary research. As literature suggests, a combination of structured and unstructured questions should be used to assess the destination image construct (Echtner and Ritchie 1993). Therefore, as proposed by Echtner and Ritchie (1993), three open questions aiming at the measurement of holistic functional, holistic psychological and unique image components were integrated in the questionnaire. In order to assess the overall image, a four point Likert-Scale was employed, asking the participants to rate their global impression of the destination from very positive to very negative. This is congruent to Baloglu and McClearlys (1999) measurement method of the overall image in their study *A model of destination image formation*. Congruently, cognitive image attributes were also tested with the help of four point Likert-Scales, reflecting different levels of agreement on attributes with regards to their adequacy for the destination Frisian Wadden Sea. The list of attributes was adapted on the basis of Pike (2009) *Destination brand positions of a competitive set of near-home destinations* since he used cognitive image factors to measure brand associations, which is also the aim of this research. Furthermore, the attribute cosy atmosphere was added to the list as an outcome of secondary research, where the cosiness of the Frisian Wadden Sea had been emphasised. In total, 14 cognitive attributes were assessed, encompassing four rather psychological factors and ten functional features. For the affective image evaluation, the two continuum scales developed by Russell and Pratt (1980) pleasant-unpleasant and sleepy-arousing were measured on a scale from one to four. As a slight adjustment, the latter scale was transformed into boring-interesting in order to not lose meaning when translating the adjectives into German. In order to gain a better understanding of the respondents´ perception of the destination, five additional scales rating psychological characteristics of the destination were adopted from the secondary study *Positie van Friesland op de Duitse vakantiemarkt* (van der Most, Peters et al.

2011). Lastly, eight unique image components that had been identified through secondary analysis were tested on a four point Likert-Scale that rated the attributes from very exceptional to very common in comparison to other coastal destinations. Moreover, the questionnaire contained questions about the travel behaviour of the respondents, enquiring whether they had already visited the Frisian Wadden Sea, their frequency of visiting and their behavioural intentions regarding likelihood of visiting within the next three years. As a conclusion of the questionnaire the socio-demographic profile of the participants was assessed by asking them to state their gender, age, family status, level of education and current Federal State of residence. The last two factors had been selected due to their influential role in the formation of the destination image (Baloglu and McCleary 1999). The questionnaire was pretested among ten persons of different age, level of education and place of residence. In consequence to their suggestions, one open question asking about symbols of the Frisian Wadden Sea was eliminated since the common perception was that this question was a repetition of the three other open questions. Furthermore, adaptations were made in the scale labelling for the question about unique image factors and the additional attribute mentality of residents was added for the same questions. Lastly, the focus of the same question as well as the ice-breaker question was narrowed down by including a comparison to other coastal destinations. For the full paper and online questionnaire see appendix 2.

5.3 Sampling

Since it is not possible to assess the destination image held by every member of the survey population, a sample was selected. The idea of sampling is to collect information about a selected test group which is representative for the entire population that is being studied. Representative samples include all characteristics defined for the examined population and reflect them in the same proportions. Findings from such samples show high external validity, thus they can be generalized to the population of focus (Veal 1997; Christensen, Johnson et al. 2011). In order to achieve representativeness, random sampling techniques are frequently applied. Random sampling implies that "all members of the population have an equal chance of inclusion in the sample" (Veal 1997, p. 205). However, due to time and budget limitations, the sample collected for this research is only partly random since it can be assumed that the respondents receiving the link via e-mail were much more likely to reside in those Federal States where the researcher had personal contacts.

Regarding the sample size, also known as *n*, this has to be determined taking into account the number of examined variables, as well as the intended degree of validity in the form of statistical confidence of the results. Furthermore, limitations such as budget and time frame of the research are key factors (Veal 1997; Long 2007; Christensen, Johnson et al. 2011). Looking at the number of variables that is being studied, according to Hoinville et al. (1977) a minimum sample size of 50 to 100 participants for each research sub-category, such as gender, income level or age group, should be examined. With respect to statistical precision, confidence intervals describe the accuracy of results from samples by stating the percent plus or minus which these findings might differ in the population. Table 2 shows the confidence intervals for a sample size of 150: As can been seen, if a percentage of 40 is drawn as a result from the sample, this value has an accuracy of plus or minus 7.8%. Thus, the true percentage of this result in the population is likely to be within 32.2% and 47.8% (Veal 1997).

Sample size	Results from sample					
	50%	40% / 60%	30% / 70%	20% / 80%	10% / 90%	5% / 95%
150	8.0	7.8	7.3	6.4	4.8	3.5

Table 2 Confidence intervals for n= 150 (Source: Veal, 1997 p.

Taking into account the number of recommended respondents for each sub-group as well as the confidence intervals and considering them with regards to time and budget restrictions the size of 200 answered questionnaires was chosen for this research.

5.4 Reliability and validity

The criteria reliability and validity serve to evaluate the quality of collected data and are therefore crucial when drawing conclusions from research findings (Babbie 2010).

Reliability has been described as "the extent to which research findings would be the same if the research were to be repeated at a later date or with a different sample of subjects" (Veal 1997, p. 35). Thus, this criteria measures whether the research methods deliver consistent results regardless of the time, place or sample under which the data has been obtained. There are four types of threats to research reliability. Firstly, the research subjects could be biased, e.g. their responses might not reflect their real opinion. Secondly, their responses might vary depending on the time and place that the observation is made. This is called subject error. Another threat to reliability is the observer error, which describes flaws in the way data is being collected. Last, observers can be biased (Finn, Elliott- White et al. 2000; Saunders, Lewis et al. 2007). Reliability in the findings of this research should be relatively high for the structured elements of the questionnaire. However, subject errors can appear during the data collection and this would lower the reliability of the results. In order to avoid subject biases, complete anonymity was assured to the survey participants.

Validity reflects to which degree the research design and measurement methods applied in a research project are appropriate to gain information about the concepts and problems that are being investigated. There are different types of validity, the most important ones being internal and external validity. Internal validity states if the effect that is being measured in the research is actually caused by the relationships that are described in the theoretical framework of the research. Therefore, it measures the extent to which the research findings are effects of the supposed causes. By contrast, external validity accounts for whether the research outcomes are universally applicable. Population validity describes the credibility of research results in reference to a wider target population and not only a selected sample (Finn, Elliott- White et al. 2000; Babbie 2010; Christensen, Johnson et al. 2011). Due to constraints in sampling methods, the research results are unlikely to be representative of the target population that is the entire German population from the age of 18 or older. Thus, while the study's external validity is likely to be rather low, efforts were made to achieve high internal validity by conducting an extensive review of relevant literature on the measurement methods of destination images, followed by a careful preparation of the questionnaire.

5.5 Data collection

The data collection took place from the 7th until the 31st of May 2012 and a total of 160 useable forms were received. Of these 134 responses were obtained from the online survey, while 26 printed questionnaires were filled in by Ameland visitors. Unfortunately the aim of n= 200 could not be reached due to relatively low response rates from the hotel guests in Ameland, where out of 130 distributed questionnaire in hotels only 10 completed forms were sent back.

5.6 Data analysis

After the data had been collected it was analysed with the help of the software *SPSS* version 18. This programme facilitates the statistical evaluation of data. The results of the open questions on image components were analysed by clustering highly similar namings into categories and subsequently calculating the frequencies of these groupings. For the structured questions, descriptive and inferential statics were used for evaluation. Descriptive statistics were employed in the form of frequency tables. These serve mainly to illustrate the findings about the destination image held by the sample (Babbie 2010). Relationships between several variables were analysed with the help of cross tabulations. Furthermore the strength of statistical associations was tested using the indicators Cramer's V for nominal variables and Kendall's tau for ordinal variables (Saunders, Lewis et al. 2009).

For the questions on cognitive, affective and unique destination characteristics the reliability test Cronbach´s alpha was used. This criterion measures the internal consistency of scales in relation to an underlying construct and therefore states the reliability of various items as indicators of a related variable (Gliem and Gliem 2003). In continuation a factor analysis was conducted for these questions in order to examine the dimensionality of the scales. The aim of this analysis is to reduce data by bundling various items into one factor or category. These extracted factors are independent of each other, but describe a common concept (Babbie 2010). The Kaiser-Meyer-Olkin Measurement of Sample Adequacy (KMO) serves as an indicator whether the common share of all variables with respect to the total variance is big enough to extract meaningful components (Baggio and Klobas 2011).

The research design outlined in this chapter served as a guideline for obtaining and adequately analysing the necessary information about destination images of the Wadden Sea. In the following, an account of the findings from primary research is given.

6 Primary research results

This overview of the primary research results contains a summary of the socio-demographic characteristics of the sample as well as frequency distributions of travel behaviour and image components. Moreover, the findings from the factor analysis and cross-tabulations are outlined. Finally, the answers to the open questions are discussed. The complete statistical results gained from the analysis are listed in appendix 3.

In total, the sample consists of 60.4% female and 39.6% male participants. When grouped into intervals of 10-years, the age distribution is as shown in table 3.

Age group	Frequency (in absolute figures)	Share (in %)
20-29	78	49.1
30-39	14	8.8
40-49	10	6.3
50-59	43	27
60-69	13	8.2
70+	1	0.6

Table 3 Age distribution of survey participants

There were 38.1% single participants, while 23.1% and 31.9% respectively claimed to be in a relationship or married. Another 3.1% were divorced and 3.8% widowed. 38.4% of the respondents were parents, whereas 61.6% did not have children. Most of the participants had a higher educational background, with 31.3% having a university entrance diploma and 43.8% a university degree. Moreover, 16.3% had attended vocational training while the rest of the sample had secondary school level certificates. When looking at the geographical distribution, the majority of the participants lived in the Federal States North Rhine-Westphalia, Bremen or Bavaria with 32.1%, 21.4% and 20.8% respectively.

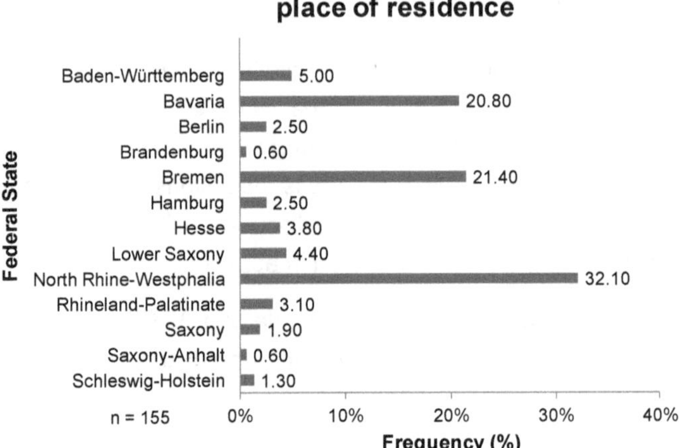

Figure 7 Place of residents of survey participants

Out of all 160 respondents, 96 had already been to the Frisian Wadden Sea. This equals 60% of the entire sample. However, when asked about the probability of visiting the Frisian Wadden Sea, the outcome was rather balanced with 51.9% of respondents stating that they were likely to travel to the destination within the next three years. Nonetheless, 30.4% were very likely to visit the destination, while only 9.5% were very improbable to do so. Therefore, the number of participants that are committed to the destination seems substantial.

The global image of the Frisian Wadden Sea resulted to be quite positive since only 10.1% of all respondents perceived the region negatively. Furthermore, 50.9% had an entirely positive image of the destination as can be seen in figure 8.

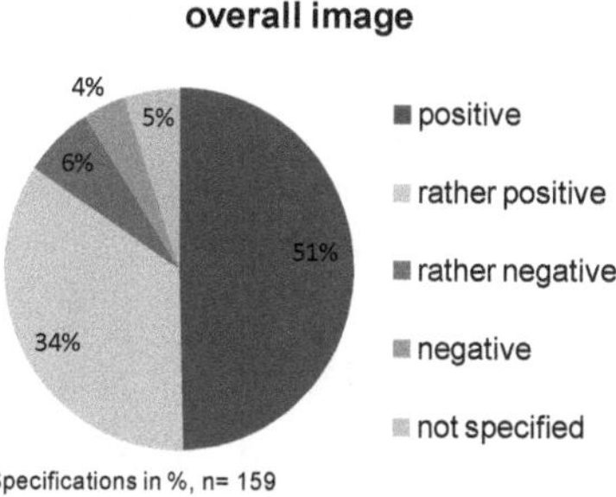

Figure 8 Overall image

In continuation, the individual image components, namely cognitive, affective and unique elements were analysed. For the cognitive elements, five attributes with an agreement-rate over 80% were identified (see figure 9). 91.9% of the participants agreed that the destination was suitable for outdoor activities and sports. Furthermore, 90.6% were of the opinion that the scenery at the destination was beautiful, while 88.2% attributed a relaxing atmosphere to the region. In addition, 81.2% of the respondents thought that the atmosphere was cosy. The destination was considered as safe by 81% of the sample. Further high ratings were given to the possibility for excursions and accessibility with 78.3% and 73.9% respectively. Moreover, the destination was considered to be child-friendly by 70% of the participants and 67% agreed that the residents of the region were friendly. Fewer respondents believed that the destination provided high quality tourism services or good value for money, with agreement rates of 60.2% and 51.9% respectively. The availability of historical and cultural sights was perceived appropriate by 42.5%. Interestingly, 41.9% of the sample regarded the destination as a crowded place with many tourists. Reciprocally, this reveals that 43.8% of the respondents consider the region as uncrowded. Lastly, only 35.6% believe that the destination offers good shopping-facilities.

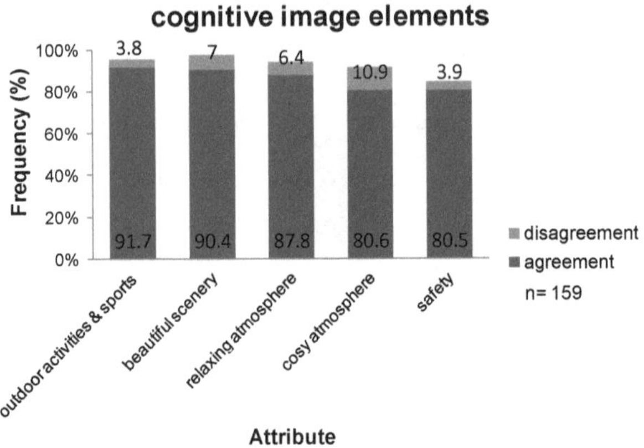

Figure 9 Highest rated cognitive image attributes

In order to explore possible underlying dimensions for the fourteen attributes that were used to measure the cognitive image, a factor analysis was conducted. Prior to this, the inner construct reliability was calculated with the help of Cronbach's alpha. The value of alpha was 0.91, which indicates that the inner consistency is very high; hence the attributes are highly adequate to measure the construct. Subsequently, two factors were extracted from the factor analysis. A KMO of 0.91 was achieved and the two factors explain 57.5% of the total variance. All attributes with loading higher than 0.6 were allocated to one of the factors (see table 4.)

The first component comprises the attributes activities and sports, relaxing atmosphere, cosy atmosphere, safety and possibility for excursions. This factor was labelled the "subjective component", because the satisfaction resulting from the attributes included in this factor can be perceived subjectively different by every individual, depending on personal motivations and attitudes. Moreover, the second component encompasses the attributes value for money, quality of touristic services, availability of sights and shopping facilities. Therefore, they represent the service component, which relates to the touristic offer of the destination and the perceived quality of its facilities. The attributes accessibility, beautiful scenery, friendly residents, child-friendliness and crowdedness were not included in any of the two factors. The reason there for could be that these attributes can be regarded either from a subjective perspective or as tangible features of the destination's offer.

	Component	
	1	2
activities and sports	,841	,087
relaxing atmosphere	,806	,299
cosy atmosphere	,804	,292
safety	,683	,252
possibility for excursions	,657	,364
accessibility	,559	,389
beautiful scenery	,544	,469
friendly residents	,542	,517
child-friendly	,535	,389
quality of touristic services	,225	,799
value for money	,185	,791
shopping facilities	,230	,702
sights	,310	,632
crowdedness	,322	,550

Table 4 Rotated component matrix of cognitive image

Since the affective image was assessed with two continuum scales, these were evaluated individually. The vast majority of participants associate some kind of pleasant feeling with the Frisian Wadden Sea, whereas by contrast only 11.9% felt unpleasant when thinking of the destination. Moreover, 59.4% relate an entirely pleasant sentiment to the destination (see figure 10). With respect to the second continuum, 71.1% considered the destination interesting in contrast to 21.4% of respondents who perceive the region as boring. However, with this element, the emotions were slightly more balanced, since a respective 41.5% and 17% regarded the Frisian Wadden Sea area as rather interesting or rather boring (see figure 11).

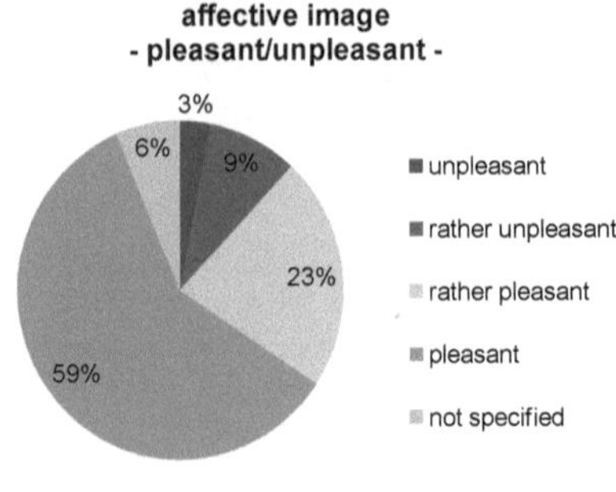

Figure 10 Affective image dimension

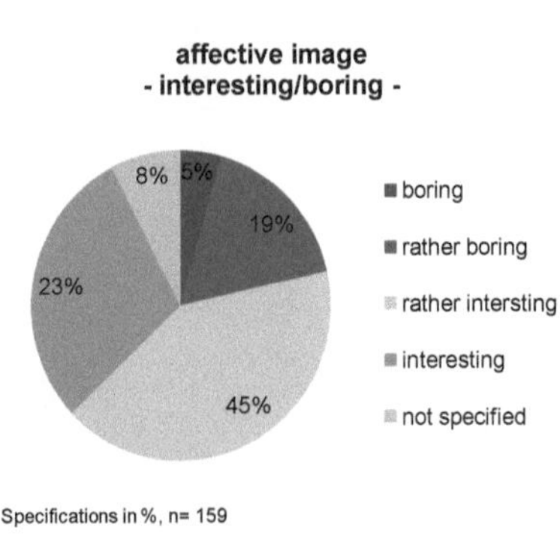

Figure 11 Affective image dimension interesting/boring

The remaining continuum scales were measuring psychological image elements in order to enhance and complement the understanding of the affective image measured with the first two scales. The destination was perceived as hospitable by 65.8%, which is rather congruent with the results from the attribute friendly residents to which 67% of the participants agreed. Moreover, 62.7% believe that the Frisian Wadden Sea area is a predictable place for holidays. In contrast, the outcome of the scale ranging from monotonous to divers was different, since a rather balanced score was achieved here. While 47.8% consider the destination as divers, 44.1% rate it as monotonous. Clear tendencies became apparent for the scales assessing the degree of luxury and modernity, with 80.9% evaluating the Frisian Wadden Sea as a frugal destination and 85.6% as traditional.

As for the cognitive image attributes, a factor analysis was also conducted for the scales measuring affective and psychological elements. The value for Cronbach's alpha was 0.74, which indicates that the inner consistency is acceptable to good. Likewise, the result for the KMO is 0.74. The factor analysis gave out two components, which account for 57.7% of the total variance. All attributes with loadings higher than 0.5 were assigned to the factors (see table 5).

	Component	
	1	2
interesting-boring	,772	,243
pleasant-unpleasant	,732	-,059
hospitable-reserved	,722	,176
divers- monotonous	,683	,366
luxurious-frugal	,094	,836
modern-traditional	,085	,798
surprising-predictable	,241	,528

Table 5 Rotated component matrix of affective and psychological image

The first component therefore includes the scales interesting-boring, pleasant-unpleasant, hospitable-reserved and divers-monotonous. This factor constitutes the sentimental evaluation of the destination in the form of feelings and subjective opinions. In contrast, the second component consists of the scales luxurious-frugal, modern-traditional and surprising-predictable. Hence, it has been denominated as "structural component", because it describes the composition of the destination in terms of psychological features.

For the unique image elements rated in the last question on the destination image of the Frisian Wadden Sea, four attributes achieved a score higher than 70%. Particularly the mudflats were rated as entirely unique by 64.6% of all respondents, while the attributes unhasty surrounding and coastal scenery were assessed as rather unique by a respective 51.9%. Furthermore, 30% regard vastness and space as a truly unique feature of the destination. Finally, the marine flora and fauna, the island feeling and the status as *UNESO* world heritage was appraised unique to some degree by more than half of the participants. Only the mentality of the residents was depicted as rather ordinary by the majority of the sample and therefore does not constitute a unique element of the destination (see figure 11).

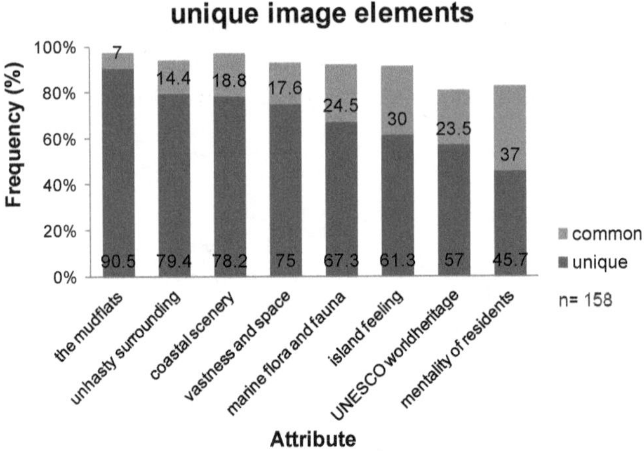

Figure 12 Unique image elements

A factor analysis was conducted after having achieved a Cronbach´s alpha of 0.84, which indicates that the inner consistency of the scales is high. However, the factor analysis revealed that the unique image is a one-dimensional construct, since only one factor was extracted. This dimension presumably refers to the uniqueness of the destination and therefore comprises all attributes included in the factor analysis.

Relationships between variables were analysed with the help of cross-tabulations (as well as correlations in the form of Cramer's V and Kendall's tau) since in many cases the number of responses per sub-group was not high enough to conduct inferential statistical tests. First, the association between the overall image and having been to the destination was examined.

		overall image				
visit		positive	rather positive	rather negative	negative	total
	yes	69	24	1	2	96
	no	12	30	9	4	55
	total	81	54	10	6	151

Table 6 Relationship overall image-visit to destination

As can be seen from table 6, visitors seem to have a more positive overall image of the Frisian Wadden See than those participants that have not been to the destination. While only three visitors had a negative global impression of the place, 13 non-visitors did not attribute it a positive image. Moreover, out of 96 visitors, 69 had an entirely positive image in comparison to 12 non-visitors.

Since the geographical distance is likely to influence destination selection as well as awareness, the relationship between visit to the destination and place of residence was investigated. Hereby, the degree of statistical association was tested in the form of Cramer´s V, which delivered a result of 0.53 and is significant at a level of 1%. Therefore, a rather strong association between the place of residence and the visitation pattern was found.

	visit			
place of residence		yes	no	total
	Baden-Württemberg	2	6	8
	Bavaria	9	24	33
	Berlin	1	3	4
	Brandenburg	0	1	1
	Bremen	22	12	34
	Hamburg	4	0	4
	Hesse	4	2	6
	Lower Saxony	6	1	7
	North Rhine-Westphalia	43	8	51
	Rhineland-Palatinate	3	2	5
	Saxony	1	2	3
	Saxony-Anhalt	1	0	1
	Schleswig-Holstein	0	2	2
	total	96	63	159

Table 7 Relationship between place of residence and visit to destination

This result is congruent with table 7 which illustrates that people living geographically close to the destination, particularly those in the bordering states Lower Saxony and North Rhine-Westphalia have visited the destination more often than participants that live in the South or East of Germany. For instance, out of 51 respondents from North Rhine-Westphalia,

43 had already been to the Frisian Wadden Sea. Moreover, six out of seven Lower Saxony residents have first-hand experience with the destination, while in contrast only nine of 33 Bavarians had travelled there.

In addition to these findings, the overall image, as well as the probability of visiting the destination, seems to be influenced by the place of residence, too. In the geographically relatively close Federal States Bremen and North Rhine-Westphalia respective 20 and 35 persons had an entirely positive image of the destination, whereas in Bavaria only nine respondents were of this opinion. However, in all Federal States with the exception of Saxony-Anhalt, there are more participants with a positive image than those with negative impressions (see appendix 4). With respect to the probability of visiting the Frisian Wadden Sea, participants from more remote Federal States were also found to be less likely to visit the destination. For instance, while in North Rhine-Westphalia 22 out of 51 participants consider that they are very probable to visit the destination within the next three years only two persons from Bavaria think so. Moreover, none of the eight respondents from Baden-Württemberg is very likely to travel to the Frisian Wadden Sea, whereas four of seven respondents from Lower Saxony intend to do so (see appendix 4). However, since the majority of the participants had a relatively positive global image, other constraints, such as accessibility are probable to influence the actual choice of destination.

The cross table relating the probability of visiting to having been to the destination delivered the result that of the 96 participants that had already been to the Frisian Wadden Sea, 45 declared it was very likely that they would visit the destination within the next three years (see appendix 4). This indicates that there is a high number of repeat visitors and this hypothesis is supported by the high frequencies of visits during the last three years that were previously described.

Furthermore, neither level of education nor age were found to considerably influence the overall image as has been proposed by Baloglu and McCleary (1999). Kendall's tau was used as an index of statistical associations between the ordinal variables overall image and level of education or age respectively. The value of tau was 0.15 for the level of education and 0.14 for the factor age at a significance level of 5%. Therefore, only a weak correlation between these factors and the overall image could be determined.

With regards to visitor profiles, the representation of certain age groups or family status at the destination was examined with cross tables. However, members of all age groups and family status categories had visited the destination and the share of participants having visited the Frisian Wadden Sea in comparison to those of the same group that had not been there was rather balanced. Hence, the destination seems to be equally popular with all ages as well as people living in any kind of marital status (see appendix 4). These results are supported by the findings that of those respondents that had visited the destination, 56% did not have children. Consequently, no clear visitor profile with regards to these socio-demographic characteristics could be established.

Lastly, for all structured questions relating to image elements, whether it is overall, cognitive, affective or unique image, non-visitors much more often chose the option "no specification" than respondents that had been to the destination. This is an indicator that the destination image is more detailed among visitors than non-visitors.

For the analysis of the open questions on functional, psychological and unique image elements, all answers were categorized and subsequently frequencies were calculated for each category. A general finding was that all 160 participants answered at least the first two of these open questions, regardless whether they had been to the destination or not. This confirms Gunn's (1988) observation that people have a mental image of a place, even if they do not have first-hand experience relating to it.

The first questions aimed to determine elements of the functional holistic image. The provided answers ranged from very specific and personal answers to general statements. The most frequent mentioned image elements can be seen in figure 13. Those answers relating to the attributes beaches and sand while including namings like long, broad, vast, sandy, beautiful beaches, as well as those referring to wind or breeze achieved top frequencies.

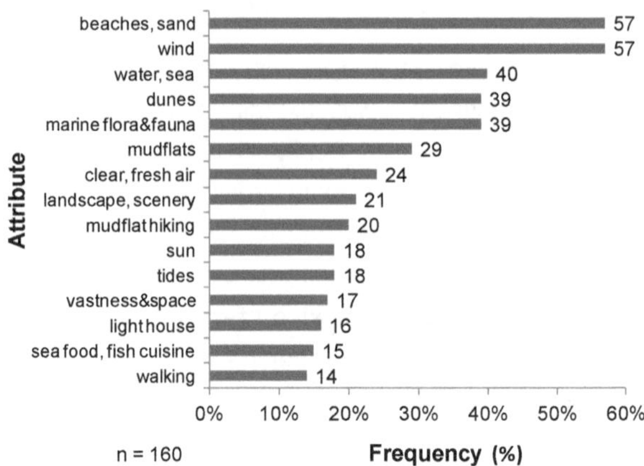

Figure 13 Most frequent elements of functional holistic image

Furthermore, most answers can be organised in five general categories. This first of these encompasses specific features of the region's landscape such as sand, beaches, water, waves, sea, dunes, mudflats, tides, dykes, vastness and space as well as salt marshes. The second group describes the marine flora and fauna, including answers as rock worm, shell, crab, shrimp, seagull and European beach grass. Another grouping combines image elements like wind, breeze, sun, rain, storm, clouds, fresh air, refreshing climate and appropriate clothing, thus characterizing climate and weather conditions at the destination. References to local characteristics such as light houses, wind mills, features of the local architecture, as well as sea food and fish cuisine constitute the fourth category. The last group deals with activities that can be realised at the destination, namely mudflat walking, (beach)-walking, biking, surfing and swimming.

Furthermore, the answers to the question on the atmosphere and mood of the destination provided rich insights to the psychological holistic image of the Frisian Wadden Sea. The four most frequent responses all dealt with the same theme, namely relaxation and recreation of mind and body (see figure 14).

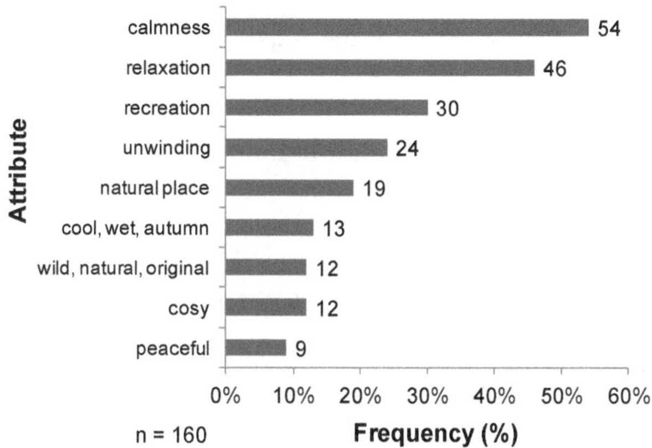

Figure 14 Most frequent elements of psychological holistic image

Although the answers cover diverse attitudes and observations, three types of replies were recognized. Firstly, there was a wide range of emotions describing the affective evaluation of the destination, e.g. boring, sad, happiness, good, pleasant, harmony. Likewise, the second category comprises psychological responses to the place in the form of unwinding, relaxation, calmness, freedom, having no limits to one's thoughts, relaxing the mind, breathing freely, liberation, letting-go and inner balance. Moreover, the majority of answers described the atmosphere at the destination with expressions like distance to daily life, traditional, clean, island-feeling, maritime, fascinating, arousing, feeling the force of nature, vastness, original, wild, rough, harsh, natural, a sense of eternity, mystic, meditative, melancholic, loneliness, uncrowded, unhasty, romantic, merrily, friendly, peaceful, cosy and hospitable.

The unique image elements reveal a broad spectrum of functional and psychological destination features. The attributes that were named with highest frequencies can be seen in figure 15. As becomes apparent from this figure, these unique image traits constitute a mixture of the previously most frequently stated functional and psychological attributes. As a matter of fact, with the exception of calmness, all of them represent functional features that are related to the natural conditions at the destination. Moreover, the *UNESCO* world heritage status of the region was recognized as a unique feature by only two participants.

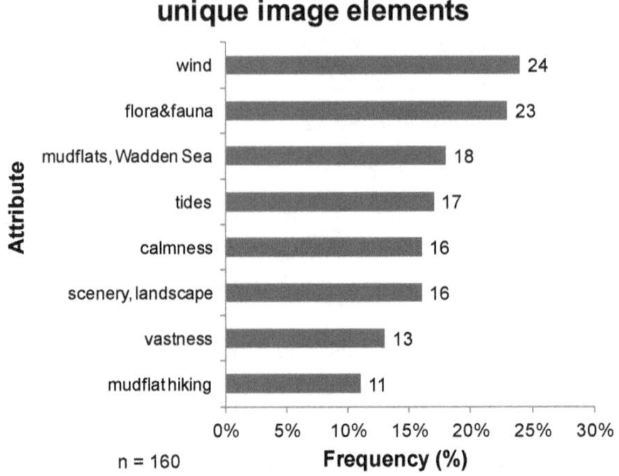

Figure 15 Most frequent elements of unique image

To sum up, the destination image of the Frisian Wadden Sea among the German source market is partly composed of a rather positive overall image, which indicates that the majority of respondents have a favourable general impression of the destination. However, when looking at the cognitive, affective and unique image elements, the perceptions are more differentiated and specific. Firstly, the cognitive image seems to be dominated by both functional and psychological features. Those characteristics that most people ascribe to the destination are good possibilities for outdoor activities and sports, beautiful scenery, a relaxing and cosy atmosphere as well as safety. Moreover, the destination is often considered as uncrowded and untouched by mass-tourism. The factor analysis revealed that there are two underlying dimensions to the cognitive image, namely a subjective and a service component. While the attributes of the first factor, with the exception of the attribute beautiful scenery, were identical with the best rated characteristics, those with the lowest evaluations can be found in the service component. It therefore seems that the natural assets and atmosphere of the Frisian Wadden Sea constitute an essential and affirmative part of the cognitive destination image among Germans. However, the quality of service and touristic facilities are perceived as rather low. This is congruent with the findings from the open question on the functional holistic image, which revealed that the main associations related to the tangible features of the region are also natural assets. Yet, these are more specific than the cognitive features of the structured question and allow for a better understanding of the mental pictures that the participants carry of the Frisian Wadden Sea. They include characteristics typical for the destination, like sand and beaches, dunes, mudflats, abundance of water, the fresh air and wind. As one can see, the destination's landscape plays a vital role in the destination image, which explains that the place is regarded as apt for outdoor activities.

Furthermore, the majority of respondents have a pleasant feeling when thinking about the Frisian Wadden Sea and they generally consider it an interesting destination. Thus, the place elicits positive emotions which result in a favourable affective image. In addition, the participants attribute the destination a rather high degree of hospitality with friendly residents. It is commonly regarded as a frugal and traditional place, which conceals few surprises. Moreover, about half of the participants believe that the destination offers diversity, while the other half describes it as monotonous. The factor analysis established that these affective and psychological destination features have both a sentimental as well as a structural dimension. With respect to the open question about psychological holistic image elements, it becomes apparent that the atmosphere and feelings associated with the destination are primarily concerned with relaxation, recreation and unwinding from the demands of daily life in a beautiful landscape. Since it is known from Baloglu and McCleary (1999) that the affective image is based on the cognitive evaluation, it can be assumed that the nature and scenery of the destination as most essential cognitive image traits inspire a relaxing and cosy atmosphere which finally result in a positive emotional experience. Moreover, since the overall image is based on these cognitive and affective components, it is also affirmative.

With regards to unique destination features, those achieving highest levels of uniqueness in the eyes of the respondents were all related to the natural qualities of the destination. For instance, the mudflats, the unhasty surrounding, the scenery, the vastness and space as well as the marine flora and fauna of the Frisian Wadden Sea were identified as fairly unique out of a given set of attributes. What is more, these features are almost entirely reflected in the most frequent responses to the open question on unique image elements. Here, the wind, the flora and fauna, the mudflats, the tides, calmness, the scenery and vastness were considered as unique by most participants. Hence, except for the attributes wind, tides and calmness, these elements are identical to the unique features of the structured question. Whereas the characteristics wind and tides are specifications of the destinations' natural conditions, calmness constitutes a psychological reaction to the unhasty surrounding. Therefore, it can be concluded that the true uniqueness of the Frisian Wadden Sea consists in its specific natural characteristics such as the mudflats, tides, wind and vastness as well as the state of mind invoked by these elements.

As for the image differences between visitors and non-visitors, the results show that non-visitors more often chose for the no-specification option than participants that had been to the destination. It can therefore be presumed that people who do not have first-hand experience with the destination have a less detailed image of the Frisian Wadden Sea. Nonetheless, all participants were able to answer at least the first of the open questions, which proofs that regardless whether persons have been to the region, they have some kind of associations with the destination. However, visitors tend to have a more positive overall image than non-visitors.

Overall, it can be said that the destination image of the Frisian Wadden Sea is dominated by the region's natural assets which constitute the common theme of all image elements and the foundation for mental imagery and associations. The significance and implications of the image identified from the primary research are discussed in the next chapter.

7 Discussion of results

In order to gain information about the sample representativeness which is a requirement for generalizing the primary research findings, the socio-demographic characteristics of the sample have to be compared to mega data of the German population (see appendix 5). Therefore, the traits gender, age, family status and place of residence were analysed with respect to their actual distribution in the German population.

While in 2010 49.1% of the Germans were male, 50.9% were female, thus the share of sexes was rather balanced. In contrast, the percentage of females in the sample of this study was 60.4 and only 39.6% of participants were male. Hence, the female gender was clearly overrepresented in the sample.

With regards to family status, 42.1% of the German population was unmarried in 2010, while 42.8% were in a marriage. Further 15.1% were either divorced or widowed. However, in the sample of this survey 31.9% were married and 61.2% were either single or living in a relationship without being wedded. The share of divorced or widowed was 6.9%. The high proportion of persons that were not married in comparison to the real distribution in the German population could be due the fact that the share of young adults under 30 accounted for 49.1% of the participants. Likewise, the under-representation of divorced or widowed could be attributed to the fact that the age group of 65 and older hardly participated in the study.

For the analysis of the age curve, the data from primary research was organised into four age groups, ranging from 15 to 24, 25 to 44, 45 to 64 and 65 years and older in order to facilitate comparison mega data from the German statistical office. Furthermore, the shares of these categories for the actual German population were recalculated to sum up to 100%. As a result it can be seen that three age groups are overrepresented in the sample, whereas the group 65 and older is clearly underrepresented with a share of 2.5% in the survey sample in comparison to 23.8% in the German society. In the age categories 25 to 44 and 45 to 64 the differences between real distribution and sample distribution are smaller than five percent, with 4.4% and 4.7% respectively. However, the share of respondents in the group of 15 to 24 year olds is twice as big then in German population. Furthermore, the youngest survey participant was 20 years old, the oldest being 70.

As for the criteria place of residence, none of the Federal States was represented in accurate portions in the sample when compared to the German population in 2010. Firstly, there were no survey participants from Saarland, Thuringia, Mecklenburg-West Pomerania. Secondly, the Federal States North Rhine-Westphalia, Hamburg, Bavaria and Bremen were overrepresented in the survey. Particularly in the case of Bremen the discrepancy is extremely high, since 0.81% of the German population lives in this Federal State. However, 21.4% of the survey respondents lived there. Moreover, with 21.8% of the German population, North Rhine-Westphalia constitutes the most populated Federal State in Germany. Yet, the percentage in the sample was 32.1 and therefore relatively higher. The remaining Federal States were underrepresented in the study. Of these Baden-Württemberg and Lower-Saxony showed differences between actual share of population and share in the survey that were higher than five percent.

In conclusion, the participants included in this primary research do not constitute a representative sample of the German population. This is to be attributed to the sampling method, which was rather non-random due to the distribution of questionnaires via e-mail. This also explains that the majority of respondents live in the Federal States Bremen, Bavaria or North Rhine-Westphalia as well as the over-representation of young adults in the sample. Due to the biased nature of the sample, several errors can occur if applying the results to the population. Therefore, it is not recommendable to generalize the findings from this survey to the German source market as a whole. Nonetheless, the answers provided by the participants are of high quality and constitute a rich pool of information on associations, perceptions and imagery related to the destination Frisian Wadden Sea. In addition to the findings from secondary research, these insights could be used to determine possible elements of a brand identity.

Having delineated the destination image gained from empirical research and examined the sample quality, the results were compared to the findings from secondary analysis in order to establish analogies and contradictions. In the first place, the overall image evaluation from the study *Imago van de Waddeneilanden* revealed that 83% of the respondents had a positive image of the Frisian Islands, while in primary analysis 85% thought likewise. These very similar results support the notion that the majority of people has a favourable global impression of the region. The attributes rated in the study *Positie van Friesland op de Duitse vakantiemarkt* can be compared to the structured question about cognitive image features in the questionnaire. Of the attributes that were comparable, three achieved rather similar values in both secondary and primary research. For instance, the attribute shopping facilities scored 31% agreement in secondary analysis, whereas in primary research a value of 34% was found. Furthermore, the existence of towns, villages and sights at the destination was considered appropriate by a respective 42%. A difference of 6% was found for the friendliness of residents. Further six characteristics were evaluated differently by the participants of the respective studies, i.e. the variation for the feature beautiful scenery is 21%. The attribute possibilities for outdoor activities and sports from primary research can be compared to the two features extensive possibilities for biking and hiking as well as ideal for active or sports holidays. While the criteria achieved the top rating of 92% in empirical research, scores of 69% and 42% respectively were identified in the secondary study. Hence, secondary research suggests that while the destination is suitable for outdoor activities like biking or hiking, it is not entirely ideal for sport holidays. Further discrepancies were identified for the features child-friendliness, service quality and value for money with variances of respectively 18%, 13% and 22%. Overall, the evaluations from secondary research tend to be less favourable than those in primary research. This could be attributed to the fact that in the secondary study, the share of visitors was 31%, while in the primary research 60% of the sample had been to the Frisian Wadden Sea. In both secondary and primary research, visitors show a strong tendency to evaluate the destination more complaisant than non-visitors. Moreover, higher agreement for subjective and natural destination features and lower values for attributes describing the service and touristic offer was found in both, primary and secondary research. Since for the assessment of the psychological image the continuum scales from the study *Positie van Friesland op de Duitse vakantiemarkt* were used in primary research, the results for this image element can be easily compared. Empirical research depicts the Frisian Wadden Sea as an interesting and hospitable destination, which is regarded as divers by some and monotonous by others. Furthermore, it is seen as a frugal and predictable destination. Similarly, secondary research findings display the region as hospitable and rather interesting. Yet, it is also considered as divers, surprising and rather luxurious, which indicates that the opinions about the structure of the destination vary from secondary to primary research. However, due to the high share of visitors with first-hand experience in the primary research sample, it can be assumed that these results are more likely to reflect the reality at the destination than those from the secondary study. The outcome from the open questions can be compared to those from spontaneous associations in all three examined image studies. Almost all attributes determined in secondary analysis also appear in primary research. For instance, characteristics related to quietude, space and nature as well as water were most frequently mentioned in the *Toerdata Noord* report. Moreover, in this study the cosy atmosphere at the destination was pointed out. In *Imago van de Waddeneilanden* the attributes coast, beaches, dunes, island feeling and space were most commonly associated with the Frisian Wadden Sea. The last of the analysed studies, *Positie van Friesland op de Duitse vakantiemarkt*, stated the mudflats, the North Sea, beaches and fresh air as most frequent namings. As apparent from this listing, the primary and most essential associations with the destination Frisian Wadden Sea all describe its natural features. This is an analogue outcome from both secondary and primary research. Finally, the holiday forms most suitable for the region that were identified in secondary analysis were enjoying nature as well as relaxing and unwinding. This supports the leading theme identified from primary research, namely that the image of the destination is mainly composed by natural assets and the notion of a relaxing atmosphere.

Overall, while many similarities between secondary and primary research were recognized, some differences also became apparent, particularly for the cognitive features and the psychological structural image. However, for the cognitive image these differences exist rather in absolute values than tendencies. Furthermore, the associations and evaluations in these secondary studies point to the same principal image theme that was detected in primary research. Therefore, the main statement resulting from the research on the image of the Frisian Wadden Sea is that its nature forms the most important source of inspiration for all kinds of perceptions, impressions, imagery and emotions related to this destination. Nature and landscape therefore constitute the core element of the region's destination image. However, this element can be further detailed when looking at the different image components. Cognitive image encompasses specific natural features such as the mudflats or characteristics of the landscape such as vastness. In addition, psychological evaluations like calmness and a relaxing atmosphere also form part of the cognitive image. As a consequence, the affective image is marked by sensations like calmness and recreation, which elicit pleasant and arousing emotional responses.

The destination image identified from primary and secondary analysis yields several consequences for destination's attractiveness and promotion. Particularly the principal image theme needs to be reflected in this light.

Since the cognitive image elements emphasize the destinations' natural qualities; it is likely to be considered appropriate for types of tourism involving outdoor activities and nature appreciation, such as eco-tourism. This has also been suggested in the study *Imago van de Waddeneilanden*. In contrast, the touristic facilities and service are perceived as below standard. This indicates that the destination's strength lies in its natural assets, whereas the touristic service constitutes a weakness. Since quality management and its communication to the target market are crucial issues, they need to be addressed in order to enhance the visitor experience. For this purpose more detailed market research is necessary to detect quality gaps between the visitors' expectations and actual performance and to elaborate appropriate solutions.

With respect to the affective image evaluation, the destination is essentially regarded as a pristine place for relaxation and recreation. Thus, it will have a high emotional appeal for those who seek calmness in order to unwind from the demands of daily life. Here again, the overall theme nature and relaxation can be found. Yet at the same time, the identified image reveals that in terms of structural psychological features, the destination is little attractive. It is seen as little surprising, glamorous or exciting and does therefore not represent a fashionable destination. Consequently, it can be concluded that the Frisian Wadden Sea will be perceived as more attractive by tourists with intrinsic motivations like relaxation and self-actualisation. By contrast, visitors with extrinsic incentives such as status are improbable to attribute the destination a favourable image.

Furthermore, the destinations' unique characteristics support the notion of the Frisian Wadden Sea as a place for nature experience and recreation in the countryside. Since almost identical features were determined from both the structured question as well as the spontaneous associations, it can be assumed that they disclose the real points of difference of the destination. Even though the *UNESCO* world heritage status was not frequently mentioned in the spontaneous associations, 28% of the respondents believed that it is a truly unique trait of the destination. By better communicating and raising awareness of this label, it could serve as a quality signal that highlights and affirms the uniqueness of the destination due to its international recognized standards.

8 Recommendations for the development of a brand identity

As a consequence of the discussed destination image, the most common associations with the Frisian Wadden Sea can be identified. In continuation, those associations that fulfil the criteria for brand associations are used for the development of a brand identity.

According to Keller's (2003) classification of brand associations, the most important image characteristics of the Frisian Wadden Sea were organised into either attribute or benefit associations. The third type of brand associations, namely brand attitudes, has not been included in this grouping since it refers to an overall evaluation of the brand which elicits favourable behavioural intentions and is therefore comparable to the overall image. Such associations cannot be included in the brand identity, because they are merely a product of effective branding. Once the brand identity has been successfully designed the brand attitude evolves as a response to brand attributes and benefits (Cai 2002). Brand attributes encompass functional and non-tangible destination features, while benefits describe personal values, motivations and benefits sought from visiting the destination (Cai 2002).

In order to reveal the nature of attribute associations, the five most popular cognitive image features of the Frisian Wadden Sea were closer examined. These were outdoor activities and sports, beautiful scenery, relaxing and cosy atmosphere as well as safety. From these five attributes in addition to the answers from the open questions, four categories of cognitive associations were found. They are either functional or psychological. The most essential cognitive associations resulting from the identified destination image are clearly related to the landscape and nature of the place. Drawing from the suggestions provided in the open question on functional holistic attributes, the elements sand, beaches and dunes, water and the sea, tides and mudflats, vastness and space as well as wind and fresh, clean air have been selected as primary scenery associations. In addition, the specific flora and fauna of the destination also invokes a multitude of associations that are included in this category. For instance, in the survey, seagulls, crabs, clams and seals frequently appeared as mental associations to the Frisian Wadden Sea. The second group refers to activity associations which include activities that are commonly associated to the destination and form part of its image. In the case of the Frisian Wadden Sea, all such activities are related to the outdoors, the strongest and most typical for the region being mudflat-hiking. With regards to atmosphere associations, this category incorporates elements from the cognitive image as well as the open question about atmosphere and mood of the Frisian Wadden Sea. Hence, the attributes relaxing, peaceful and cosy were prevalently found to describe the atmosphere at the destination. Lastly, subjective structural associations are those that involve a psychological evaluation of the destination's intangible characteristics. In this sense, the Frisian Wadden Sea is commonly regarded as a welcoming and hospitable destination. Since it has not developed mass-tourism structures and the landscape is vast, it is also perceived as uncrowded. Moreover, due to the absence of mass-tourism and the low degree of urbanisation which implies a rather slow pace of life, the destination is considered traditional. Finally, the visitors are of the opinion that the destination is safe.

On the basis of these specific brand attributes, matching brand benefits can be determined. The responses from the open questions form an important source of information about benefits and motivations associated with the Frisian Wadden Sea, however, further associations could be deduced from the previously described attributes. The principal motivation for visiting the Frisian Wadden Sea is recreation. Consequently, the most popular benefit associations are calmness, relaxation and unwinding by leaving the demands and stress of daily life behind. As previously laid out, the vastness, uncrowdedness and natural beauty of the destination create a relaxing and peaceful atmosphere which itself forms the basis for the described benefits. Furthermore, these experienced benefits elicit pleasant and arousing emotional responses. Another type of benefit association could be the sensation of safety. In a complex world, with the threat of terrorist attacks and political unrests, safety has become a major decisive factor for the choice of destination and this trend is estimated to continue (European Travel Commission 2006). Thus, the sensation of safety could be an important benefit association, especially for insecure travellers that prefer to visit destinations with a high degree of familiarity. This is supported by the common perception that the experience at the destination is rather predictable, which further appeals to tourists in search of recreation.

Having identified the most likely brand associations in the form of attitude and benefit association related to the Frisian Wadden Sea, these need to be evaluated with regards to Keller's (2003) criteria for brand associations. He argues that all associations need to be strong, favourable and unique in order to contribute to the creation of brand equity. Hence, all associations which are to be incorporated in the brand identity need to fulfil these requirements. All of the selected associations are strong, because they are the image elements that most frequently appeared in primary and secondary research and must therefore represent central perceptions for the majority of participants. Furthermore, the associations are considered as favourable because they conclude in a positive overall evaluation of the destination in the form of an affirmative global image. Hence, since the chosen attitude and benefit associations are the cognitive and affective image elements that compose this positive holistic image, they are also likely to be favourable. However, for the criteria uniqueness, the associations need to be reflected with regards to the findings on unique destination features. The natural assets such as the landscape with mudflats and tides, the vastness of the place and the coastal scenery as well as the activity mudflat-walking have been rated as truly unique in the primary research. However, the relaxing and cosy atmosphere is likely to be a strong and favourable association, yet not exclusive to the Frisian Wadden Sea. The same applies for the associations related to the psychological structure of the destination. However, atmosphere associations arise as a consequence of the described natural qualities of the destination, which is why they are rooted in a unique setting and are therefore also exceptional.

The associations of safety and hospitality, uncrowdedness and tradition do not constitute unique elements. However, the attributes uncrowdedness and tradition support the notion of a spacious destination with a relaxing atmosphere and are therefore important associations. With respect to the benefit associations, the calmness at the destination has been voted as unique, which is why it can be assumed that all associations related to the ability to relax and unwind at the Frisian Wadden Sea are somehow also specifically related to the destination. As for safety, even though being a strong and favourable association, it does not constitute a unique feature. Those brand associations that are at the same time strong, favourable and unique are all related to the principal theme of the destination image, being the natural qualities and the emotional and psychological benefits drawn from their appreciation.

In the next step, the possible brand associations are used for the creation of a brand identity by first establishing the six-level brand pyramid and subsequently selecting the core values and elements of the brand. As known from destination branding theory, the six level brand pyramid is a tool to develop a brand identity on the basis of brand associations by organising these on several levels and narrowing them down to the very essence of the brand that is the brand identity (UNWTO 2009).

Attributes that describe the destination constitute the foundation of the pyramid. In the case of the Frisian Wadden Sea the selected associations are related to the nature and atmosphere at the destination, which consequently refer to the principal image theme. Natural assets are depicted in the form of the three elements water, air and land. Furthermore, the marine fauna fills the living space Wadden Sea with life. The Wadden Sea itself and its waves represent the main water associations. Those associations alluding to the element land comprise the features sand, dunes and broad beaches. Moreover, the clear, fresh marine air and the wind are characteristics of the aerial qualities of the destination. The most central nature association are the mudflats that stretch as far as the eye can see and add a sense of vastness to the landscape. The ever changing high and low tides which create this specific environment are further crucial destination features, while the marine fauna that is found in the mudflats embodies the exceptional living conditions in this unique living space in-between water and land. The most typical and widely know marine animals of this region are crabs, mussels, rock worms, sea gulls and seals. Besides nature associations, atmosphere related destination attributes are those of a slow-paced and uncrowded destination. This builds the basis for the notion of an unhasty and calming ambience. Additionally, the region is depicted as traditional, which implies that it is not affected by the hectic bustle of modern urban life and that the structure of the destination is original in the sense that it has not been altered by modern constructional features.

The second level of the pyramid comprises rational benefits that can be gained from visiting the destination. Drawing from the attribute associations described for the first level, the main benefit offered by the Frisian Wadden Sea exists in its unspoilt nature and unique scenic beauty. Due to the low impact of human activities on the landscape, the environment is pure and unpolluted and therefore constitutes a healthy surrounding. Consequently, extensive opportunities for nature experience in the form of outdoor activities such as mudflat hiking account for tangible highlights of the destination. Due to the described natural qualities and the absence of mass tourism further value in the form of a tranquil and peaceful character is added to the region.

Building upon rational benefits, emotional benefit associations constitute the subsequent step towards the identification of core brand elements. As the Frisian Wadden Sea has been characterized as a prime destination for relaxation and recreation on the basis of nature enjoyment, emotional associations of actual and potential visitors congruently allude to this central theme. Thus, the prospect to unwind and find calmness in the unhasty environment of the destination are principal advantages related to the region. The wish to leave behind the pressures of daily life and the idea to experience the vastness of the mudflats reflected in one's mind result in the notion of a clear mind. This association confers the destination the status of a place where no limits are put to one's thoughts, essentially embodying a space where ideas drift freely and new sources of inspiration and energy will be found.

The brand personality acts as an intermediate stage between benefit associations and the upper levels of the brand pyramid which compose the brand identity. At this stage, the key brand associations are determined on the basis of brand benefits and are subsequently broken down to reveal the very essence of the future brand (UNWTO 2009). Drawing from the identified rational and emotional brand benefits of the Frisian Wadden Sea, it becomes apparent that the true uniqueness of the destination consists in one particular natural characteristic, namely the mudflats. This landscape embodies both rational qualities like a world-wide unique environment and emotional benefits such as detachment from the preoccupations of daily life. Hence, the mudflats constitute the core imagery element of the destination brand Frisian Wadden Sea. The distinctiveness of this natural asset exists not in the fact that it belongs to the largest tidal area of the world, but mainly in the phenomenon of its formation. This is a process during which water becomes land and land is resumed by the sea. Moreover, the vastness of landscape produces the effect that the borders between land, water and sky are blurred, blending them together at a distant horizon. The mudflat is therefore a hybrid environment that is composed by the fusion of the elements water, land and air which are drawn together and harmonized by the laws of physics. The tidal range is the visual expression of this continuous interplay between the elements, which exposes the mudflats in regular intervals of 12 hours following the rhythm of nature. It is therefore a place where the forces of nature can be visually observed under natural conditions and one has the possibility to witness the spectacle of creation. Since this process has not been altered by mankind, but is entirely natural, it appeals to the longing to reconnect to the origins of life and experience oneself as a natural being that is commonly shared by many members of Western societies as a response to the rush of modern life. Therefore, the mudflats are powerful associations and serve as a symbol for the character of the destination brand.

The penultimate stage of the branding pyramid considers the brand values. These are vital for the brand identity, because they built the value structure of the brand that forms part of the brand identity (UNWTO 2009). As gathered from the brand personality, the merit of the destination Frisian Wadden Sea is to be found in its mudflats, which reflect at the same time environmental and aesthetic qualities and more important, an abstract psychological connotation by alluding to the constant change of tides as a process of creation that is fuelled by the forces of nature. The values of the destination brand Frisian Wadden Sea have to be aligned and interpreted in this sense in order to enhance the brand with relevant significance. When analysing the symbolism of the brand personality, three value propositions can be determined. Firstly, mudflats are intact and natural because they have not been modified by human activities and therefore present themselves in a pristine condition as created by nature. This should be reflected in the brand values as a kind of authenticity which can only derive from nature itself and stands for a pure and original character. This value is best expressed by the German term "Ursprünglichkeit", since it implies naturalness and the conservation of an original state. The second brand value refers to the relationship of the elements water, land and wind which is ultimately responsible for the hybrid nature of the mudflats. These elements are extremely divers, yet they are linked through the tidal range which fuses them in harmony and gives rise to the unique environment of the mudflats. This process of diversity becoming unity is possible due to an interconnectedness that is omnipresent in nature. All elements and processes of nature are interlinked and these components, including human beings, form part of a greater entity that is the eco-system Earth itself. In this eco-system, the forces of nature arrange all components in a way that minimizes attrition and often results in a coalition of elements. Since this truth is often forgotten in modern life, the mudflats are a strong reminder of the fact that the aspiration of unity despite differences creates powerful synergies and is therefore a crucial value in both, natural and human social life. Finally, the third brand value is related to the continuous change of tides that occurs in fixed intervals. Since this perpetual cycle is only amenable to the laws of physics, it epitomises the rhythm of nature. This has twofold consequences as on one hand it evokes a sense of eternity in the observer that is awe-inspiring. On the other hand, it implies that the destination functions at its own pace, which is distinct from the fast pace of life that dominates most Western societies. These associations reinforce the first brand value by enhancing the notion of a pure and original destination. Moreover, they enrich the brand with an essential meaning, since many persons feel the desire to disconnect from their hectic lives and retrieve a sense of calmness that can be found in the pace of nature.

Having identified adequate brand values, the core elements of the brand are to be selected. They comprise the timeless essence of the brand and are therefore a central part of the brand identity (UNWTO 2009). The motive of change between mudflats and water insinuate that the destination is rooted in the rhythm of nature. The range of tides is a continuous process during which the mudflats arise out of the waters of the Wadden Sea and are subsequently re-flooded. It therefore represents an eternal circle in the course of which composition and decomposition take place due to a fusion of elements that is driven by the forces of nature. However, even though this process of formation and separation is perpetually repeated, the emerging mudflats are never exactly the same as they have been during previous low tides due to the forces of sedimentation and corrosion. Hence, there is also a constant innovation in the environment. This continuous striving towards something new contains an element of creativity and is a fundamental characteristic of creation. Furthermore, the decomposition of landscape that occurs at every change of tides also forms part of the creation process, as it creates space for something new. Given that the progress towards renewal is infinite, creation can be regarded as a continuous, never finishing cycle. It represents the very cycle of life that becomes visualized in the range of tides of the Frisian Wadden Sea, which constantly repeats itself in the course of approx. 12 hours. However, even though the act of creation can be witnessed at the destination, there is a mystic and metaphysical aspect to the process that cannot by seized by the rational parts of the human mind, but which appeals to the spirituality of the human soul. It conveys a sense of transcendence to the observer, who is inspired and spiritually enriched by this awe-inspiring experience. Hence, the core essence of the Frisian Wadden Sea exists in the eternal myth of creation. Figure 16 illustrates the brand pyramid for the Frisian Wadden Sea as previously described.

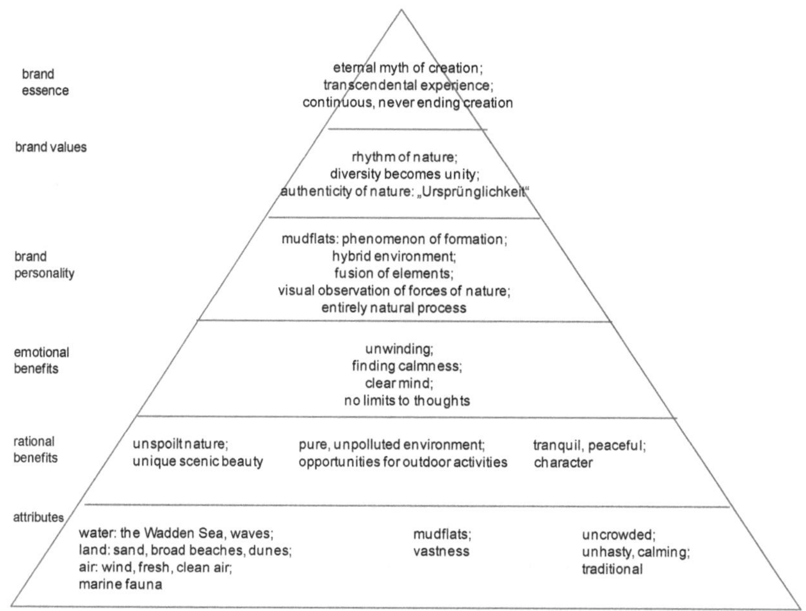

Figure 16 Branding pyramid of the Frisian Wadden Sea

On the basis of the brand pyramid, the brand identity is established. Aaker´s (1996, p.68) definition of brand identity as “a unique set of associations that the brand strategist aspires to create and maintain” as well as the *UNWTO*´s (2009) suggestion that the brand identity is composed of both brand values and essence serve as a theoretical foundation for the selection of the identity elements. The core aspect of the brand identity for the destination brand Frisian Wadden Sea is thus the powerful association of a continuous, infinite act of creation that is rooted in a fusion of elements. Due to the spiritual qualities of this process, it embodies the eternal myth of creation that involves a sensation of transcendence. The values that the brand identity encompasses reflect the spirit of creation, the first of these being the authenticity of nature. This value is best portrayed by the German expression “Ursprünglichkeit”, which represents the main traits of creation, namely the originality, pureness and innovation that are essential to the act. Another value is conveyed in the transformation from diversity into unity that is an underlying principle to the process of creation. Lastly, creation operates at its own pace which is equal to the rhythm of nature and this implies that the brand itself has an individual and natural pace.

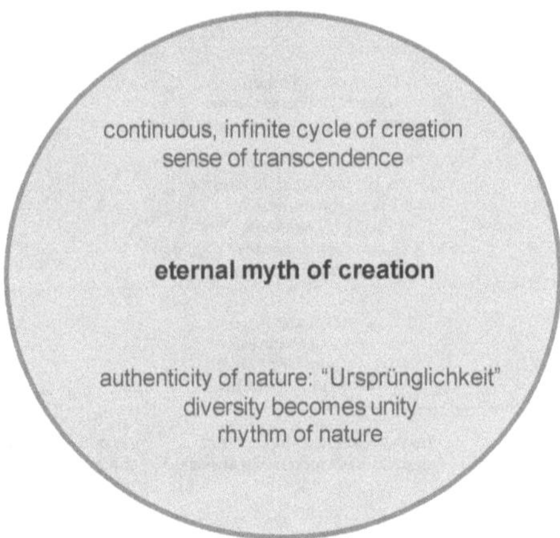

Figure 17 Brand identity of the Frisian Wadden Sea

The virtue of the hereby identified and outlined brand identity for the destination brand Frisian Wadden Sea lies in the power of its allegory. The act of creation is one of the great myths of existence, since it marks the very beginning of the latter and has been present since the birth of the universe. Nevertheless, it still continues and will do so eternally. It is therefore something magnificent and yet unexplainable, because it reaches beyond the capacity of the human mind. For this reason humans are struck with awe at the direct encounter with the process of creation. It is a strong reminder that humans, though being a highly advanced being, still form part of the natural cycle of life. This realisation puts one´s own life into a greater perspective and serves to fill the observer with amazement at the wonders of nature. This sensation appeals to the prevalent desire to detach from the preoccupations of daily life and regain inner balance by returning to a more natural way of life, which is commonly felt by persons living in fast paced societies. When experiencing the spiritual inspiration deriving from the transcendence of creation, one feels deeply connected to the origins of life. In addition, the notion of "Ursprünglichkeit" and the idea that diversity can be fused into unity in a peaceful way are both values that have become almost extinguished in modern life, which is why they have a strong attraction. The brand identity of the Frisian Wadden Sea therefore comprises a set of elements and values that combine high emotional value and relevance for the target group by evoking not only cognitive or emotional associations, but by alluding to latent desires.

9 Conclusion

The findings of this research have resulted in recommendations for the development of a brand identity for the Frisian Wadden Sea. From an academic point of view this process of identity development has been based on theoretical concepts and scientific techniques such as quantitative methods and analytic deduction and is therefore an account of the status quo in tourism research. From a practitioner's perspective the determined identity proposition is a promising foundation for building a strong destination brand. Since the identity constitutes the timeless essence of a brand, it will influence all further steps of branding including strategy development and implementation. Moreover, the brand identity should be integrated in all actions and communications to the target market in order to ensure that the spirit of the brand is transmitted (UNWTO 2009). With regards to the branding process, after having developed a brand identity, this core essence has to be enhanced with meaning for the target audience (Keller 2003). This step in the branding process refers to the brand positioning. It involves a selection of some elements of the identity that will be highlighted to the target group. At this stage, the brand is to be differentiated from competitors with the help of unique selling propositions (USP). Aaker (1991, p. 190f.) defines USPs as a "specific and unique product benefit important enough to affect consumer purchases". A USP therefore endows a brand with a competitive advantage by emphasising a unique quality that competitors cannot provide (Keller 2003). In the case of the Frisian Wadden Sea, the USP can be found in the brand identity itself. The opportunity to visually observe the spectacle of creation and to experience the transcendence that is concealed in the eternal mysteries of this process is what makes the destination unique and is therefore its strongest USP. The active communication of this point of difference should be the focus of the marketing action plan that is to be elaborated during later stages of the brand building process. The correct implementation of this USP has high potential to elicit positive brand responses by adding value to the destination. Once the brand has been established and grown strong, the brand image should be used to influence the destination image. In consequence, the destination´s attractiveness will increase both, among potential tourists and actual visitors who are likely to experience their visit more consciously in the light of the branding theme.

Furthermore, the branding efforts could be supported by the UNSECO world heritage status of the Wadden area, since some components of the brand identity are similarly described in the report for the nomination of the area. For instance, the motive of a hybrid environment and the fusion of elements is reflected in the area description when it says that "land lies in water and the sea moves over water" (CWSS 2008p. 21). Moreover, the vastness of the tidal wetlands is pointed out as a unique feature of the landscape and it is mentioned that the "tidal areas remained very much product of natural interplay between a shallow sea and a flat land" (CWSS 2008, p.27). Thus, the notion of an authentic and pure destination that possesses an environment that is changing according to the forces of nature is confirmed by the *UNESCO* authorities. As a consequence, the *UNESCO* status could be integrated in the branding strategies and serve as a quality signal as well as to raise awareness.

However, the brand identity identified from the destination image of the German source market only considers the perspective of outsiders. In order to gain full comprehension of the perceptions held about the destination and to complete the picture derived from secondary and primary research, the destination image among residents and other stakeholders needs to be examined. As known from tourism theory, the differences between projected and perceived destination image has to be analysed and gaps should be closed in order to ensure that the visitors´ expectations are met with adequate experiences (Tasci and Kozak 2006; Qu, Kim et al. 2011). Therefore, the brand identity of the Frisian Wadden Sea as outlined in this study should be complemented with insights and opinions of the local population.

Even though this research has attempted to keep to scientific standards throughout the process, there are several limitations to the study that the readers should be aware of. In the first place, the sample was biased with regards to the socio-demographic indicators gender, age, level of education and place of residence due to constraints in the sampling method. The sample was collected using e-mail distribution which does not qualify as non-random sampling. Hence, the findings drawn from the sample are not representative of the survey population. Secondly, the sample size was rather small, which is why the number of cases in several sub-groups was too small to conduct valid statistical tests and the results from the indicators Cramer V and Kendall tau lack validity. Nevertheless the researcher chose to employ them in order to examine tendencies. Overall, a market research using standardized sample techniques and collecting a larger sample is advisable in order to verify the findings of this research.

Moreover, there are further fields of investigation and action that could prove beneficial for the destination. Research on constraints to destination attractiveness is indicated in order to better understand why visitors that have a positive destination image of the Frisian Wadden Sea do not chose for this destination for their holidays. Furthermore, awareness of the destination particularly in those German Federal States that are geographically more distanced from the destination needs to be raised with the help of marketing campaigns. Lastly, the image of the destination should be improved in the aspects of service and quality of touristic facilities since it was perceived as sub-standard by the majority of survey participants.

References

Aaker, D. A. (1991). Management des Markenwertes, Frankfurt, Campus Verlag.

Aaker, D. A. (1996). Building Strong Brands, London, Simon & Schuster UK Ltd.

Aaker, D. A. and J. G. Shansby (1982). "Positioning your product." Business Horizons **25**(3): 56-62.

Ahmed, Z. U. (1991). "The influence of the components of a state's tourist image on product positioning strategy." Tourism Management **12**(4): 331-340.

Babbie, E. (2010). The Practice of Social Research. 13th eds., Canada, Wadsworth CENGAGE Learning.

Baggio, R. and J. Klobas (2011). Quantitative Methods in Tourism- A Handbook, Bristol, Channel View Publications.

Baloglu, S. and D. Brinberg (1997). "Affective Images of Tourism Destinations." Journal of Travel Research **35**(4): 11-15.

Baloglu, S. and K. W. McCleary (1999). "A model of destination image formation." Annals of Tourism Research **26**(4): 868-897.

Beerli, A. and J. D. Martín (2004). "Factors influencing destination image." Annals of Tourism Research **31**(3): 657-681.

Byon, K. K. and J. J. Zhang (2010). "Development of a scale measuring destination image." Marketing Intelligence & Planning **28**(4): 508 - 532.

Cai, L. A. (2002). "Cooperative branding for rural destinations." Annals of Tourism Research **29**(3): 720-742.

CBS. (2012). "Bevolkingsontwikkeling; regio per maand." Retrieved 21/05/2012, from http://statline.cbs.nl/StatWeb/publication/default.aspx?DM=SLNL&PA=37230NED&D1=0%2c18%2c20%2c22&D2=0%2c5-16%2c101-630&D3=130&HDR=G2%2cT&STB=G1&VW=D.

Chen, C.-F. and D. Tsai (2007). "How destination image and evaluative factors influence behavioral intentions?" Tourism Management **28**: 1115-1122.

Christensen, L. B., R. B. Johnson, et al. (2011). Research Methods, Design, and Analysis. 11th eds., Boston, Pearson.

Crompton, J. L. (1979). "An Assessment of the Image of Mexico as a Vacation Destination and the Influence of Geographical Location Upon That Image." Journal of Travel Research **17**(4): 18-23.

Crompton, J. L., P. C. Fakeye, et al. (1992). "Positioning: The Example of the Lower Rio Grande Valley in the Winter Long Stay Destination Market." Journal of Travel Research **31**(2): 20-26.

CWSS (2008). Nomination of the Dutch-German Wadden Sea as World Heritage Site- Volume One. Wilhelmshaven, Common Wadden Sea Secretariat.

CWSS. (n.a.). "Wadden Sea World Heritage." Retrieved 21/05/2012, from http://www.waddensea-worldheritage.org/wadden-sea-world-heritage.

de Haas, M. and P. H. Huig (2010). Consumentenonderzoek Toerisme. Leeuwarden, Stenden Instituut Service Management.

De Leeuw, E. D. and J. J. Hox (2011). Internet surveys as part of a mixed-mode design. Social and Behavioral Research and the Internet. M. Das, P. Ester and L. Kaczmirek. New York, Routledge: 45-76

de Rijk, F. and H. Borger (2008). Image Onderzoek Waddeneinlanden- Detailrapport. Eersel, Stichting Waddenfederatie te Leeuwarden.

Die Nordsee GmbH. (n.a.). "die Nordsee." Retrieved 24/05/2012, from http://www.die-nordsee.de/.

Echtner, C. M. and J. R. B. Ritchie (1993). "The Measurement of Destination Image: An Empirical Assessment." Journal of Travel Research **31**(4): 3-13.

Echtner, C. M. and J. R. B. Ritchie (2003). "The Meaning and Measurement of Destination Image." The Journal of Tourism Studies **14**(1): 37- 48.

ETFI. (2012). "Toerdata Noord." Retrieved 12/05/2012, from http://etfi.eu/toerdata.

European Travel Commission (2006). Tourism Trends in Europe. Bruxelles, European Travel Commission.

Fakeye, P. C. and J. L. Crompton (1991). "Image Differences between Prospective, First-Time, and Repeat Visitors to the Lower Rio Grande Valley." Journal of Travel Research **30**(2): 10-16.

Finn, M., M. Elliott- White, et al. (2000). Tourism & Leisure Research Methods- Data collection, analysis and interpretation, Harlow, Pearson Education Limited.

Gallarza, M. G., I. G. Saura, et al. (2002). "Destination image: Towards a Conceptual Framework." Annals of Tourism Research **29**(1): 56-78.

Gartner, W. C. (1989). "Tourism Image: Attribute Measurement of State Tourism Products Using Multidimensional Scaling Techniques." Journal of Travel Research **28**(2): 16-20.

Gliem, J. A. and R. R. Gliem (2003). Calculating, Interpreting, and Reporting Cronbach's Alpha Reliability Coefficient for Likert-Type Scales. 2003 Midwest Research to Practice Conference in Adult, Continuing, and Community Education. Columbus, Ohio: 82-88.

Gunn, C. A. (1988). Vacationscapes: Designing tourist regions. 2nd eds., New York, Van Nostrand Reinhold.

Hoinville, G., R. Jowell, et al. (1977). Survey Research Practice, London, Heinemann.

Hu, Y. and J. R. B. Ritchie (1993). "Measuring Destination Attractiveness: A Contextual Approach." Journal of Travel Research **32**(2): 25-34.

Hunt, J. D. (1975). "Image as a Factor in Tourism Development." Journal of Travel Research **13**(3): 1-7.

Keller, K. L. (2003). Strategic Brand Management- Building, Measuing, and Managing Brand Equity. 2nd eds., Upper Saddle River, New Jersey, Pearson Education International.

Kim, D. and R. R. Perdue (2011). "The Influence of Image on Destination Attractiveness." Journal of Travel & Tourism Marketing **28**(3): 225-239.

Kim, H. and S. L. Richardson (2003). "Motion picture impacts on destination images." Annals of Tourism Research **30**(1): 216-237.

Koniklijk Nederlands Meteorologisch Instituut. (n.a.). "Langjarige gemiddelden en extremen, tijdvak 1971 - 2000." Retrieved 16/05/2012, from http://www.knmi.nl/klimatologie/normalen1971-2000/gemiddelde_maandtemperatuur_jul_dec.html.

Kotler, P. (2003). A Framework for Marketing Management. 2nd eds., Upper Saddle River, New Jersey, Pearson Education Inc.

Kotler, P. and G. Armstrong (2004). Principles of Marketing. 10th eds., Upper Saddle River, New Jersey, Pearson Education Inc.

Long, J. (2007). Researching Leisure, Sport and Tourism- The essential guide, London, SAGE Publications Ltd.

Lovelock, C. and J. Wirtz (2004). Services Marketing- People, Technology, Strategy. 5th eds., Upper Saddle River, New Jersey, Pearson Education Inc.

Mansfeld, Y. (1992). "From motivation to actual travel." Annals of Tourism Research **19**(3): 399-419.

Morgan, N. (2002). "New Zealand, 100% Pure. The creation of a powerful niche destination brand." Brand Management **9**(4-5): 335- 354.

Morgan, N., A. Pritchard, et al. (2004). destination branding- creating the unique destinaton proposition. 2nd eds., Oxford, Elsevier Butterworth-Heinemann.

Mostert, M. (2001). Frisians. The Blackwell Encyclopaedia of Anglo-Saxon England. M. Lapidge. Oxford, Blackwell: 195f.

n.a. (2012). "Find your GPS Coordinates." Retrieved 16/05/2012, from http://www.longitude-latitude-maps.com/city/151_15,Ameland,Friesland,Netherlands.

NBTC (2008). Destinatie Holland 2020- Toekomstvisie Inkomend Toerisme. Assendelft, Nederlands Bureau voor Toerisme & Congressen (NBTC), afdeling Onderzoek.

Phelps, A. (1986). "Holiday destination image — the problem of assessment: An example developed in Menorca." Tourism Management **7**(3): 168-180.

Pike, S. (2009). "Destination brand positions of a competitive set of near-home destinations." Tourism Management **30**(6): 857-866.

Qu, H., L. H. Kim, et al. (2011). "A model of destination branding: Integrating the concepts of the branding and destination image." Tourism Management **32**(3): 465-476.

Russell, J. A. and G. Pratt (1980). "A Description of the Affective Quality Attributed to Environments." Journal of Personality and Social Psychology **38**(2): 311-322.

Russell, J. A., L. M. Ward, et al. (1981). "Affective Quality Attributed to Environments." Environment and Behavior **13**(3): 259-288.

San Martín, H. and I. A. Rodríguez del Bosque (2008). "Exploring the cognitive–affective nature of destination image and the role of psychological factors in its formation." Tourism Management **29**(2): 263-277.

Saunders, M., P. Lewis, et al. (2007). Research Methods for Business Students. 4th eds., Harlow, Pearson Education Limited.

Saunders, M., P. Lewis, et al. (2009). Research methods for business students. 5th eds., Harlow, Pearson Education Limited.

Sirgy, M. J. and C. Su (2000). "Destination Image, Self-Congruity, and Travel Behavior: Toward an Integrative Model." Journal of Travel Research **38**(4): 340-352.

Statistics Netherlands. (2012). "Guests in leisure accommodations; by country of residence and region." Retrieved 12/03/2012, from http://statline.cbs.nl/StatWeb/publication/?DM=SLEN&PA=70021ENG&D1=1-2,4-12,15-18&D2=a&D3=50,135,220&LA=EN&HDR=T&STB=G1,G2&VW=T.

Tasci, A. D. A. and W. C. Gartner (2007). "Destination Image and Its Functional Relationships." Journal of Travel Research **45**(4): 413-425.

Tasci, A. D. A., W. C. Gartner, et al. (2007). "Conceptualization and Operationalization of Destination Image." Journal of Hospitality & Tourism Research **31**(2): 194-223.

Tasci, A. D. A. and M. Kozak (2006). "Destination brands vs destination images: Do we know what we mean?" Journal of Vacation Marketing **12**(4): 299-317.

Toerdata Noord (2010). Open vragen Verblijfstoeristen Toerdata Noord. Microsoft Excel. O. v. V. T. Noord. Leeuwarden, Stenden Instituut Service Management.

Um, S. and J. L. Crompton (1990). "Attitude determinants in tourism destination choice." Annals of Tourism Research **17**(3): 432-448.

UNWTO (1980). Tourist images, Madrid, World Tourism Organisation.

UNWTO (2009). Handbook on Tourism Destination Branding, Madrid, World Tourism Organisation, European Travel Commission.

UNWTO (2011). UNWTO Tourism Highlight- 2011 Edition. Madrid, World Tourism Organisation.

van der Most, K., L. Peters, et al. (2011). Positie van Friesland op de Duitse vakantiemarkt. n.a., Nederlands Bureau voor Toerisme & Congressen- Afdeling Onderzoek.

Veal, A. J. (1997). Research Methods for Leisure and Tourism- A Practical Guide. Harlow, Pearson Education Limited.

APPENDIX

1 Questionnaire

Paper format questionnaire

Fragebogen Image des Reiseziels friesisches Wattenmeer

Als Studentin des Internationalen Studienganges Tourismusmanagement an der Hochschule Bremen führe ich in Zusammenarbeit mit dem European Tourism Futures Institute in den Niederlanden eine Bachelorarbeit zum Thema Image des Reiseziels friesisches Wattenmeer durch.
Dies umfasst alle Vorstellungen, Gefühle und Bilder, die Sie mit dem Reiseziel friesisches Wattenmeer verbinden. Diese Region liegt im Nordwesten der Niederlande und erstreckt sich sowohl entlang der Küste der holländischen Provinz Friesland, sowie über die Westfriesischen Inseln Vieland, Terschelling, Ameland, und Schiermonnikoog.
Im Rahmen dieses Projektes würde ich Sie bitten, einige Fragen über das genannte Reiseziel zu beantworten. Selbstverständlich werden Ihre Daten anonym verarbeitet. Vielen Dank für Ihre Mitarbeit!

I Reiseverhalten

1. Was ist Ihr liebstes Küstenreiseziel?

____

2. Haben Sie schon einmal eine Reise an das friesische Wattenmeer unternommen?
O ja O nein *(weiter bei Frage 4)*

3. Wie oft haben Sie in den letzten drei Jahren das friesische Wattenmeer bereist? ______

4. Wie hoch ist die Wahrscheinlichkeit, dass Sie in den nächsten drei Jahren eine Reise an das friesische Wattenmeer unternehmen werden?

O sehr wahrscheinlich O wahrscheinlich O unwahrscheinlich O sehr unwahrscheinlich

II Reiseziel friesisches Wattenmeer

5. Welche Eigenschaften oder Bilder fallen Ihnen ein, wenn sie an das Reiseziel friesisches Wattenmeer denken? (gerne in Stichworten)

____

____

6. Wie würden Sie die Atmosphäre oder Stimmung, die Sie mit dem Reiseziel friesisches Wattenmeer verbinden, beschreiben? (gerne in Stichworten)

____

____

7. Bitte nennen Sie charakteristische oder einzigartige Merkmale, die Sie mit dem friesischen Wattenmeer verbinden. (gerne in Stichworten)

____

____

8. Bitte beurteilen Sie den Gesamteindruck, den Sie vom Reiseziel friesisches Wattenmeer haben.

positiv	eher positiv	eher negativ	negativ	keine Angabe
O	O	O	O	O

9. Bitte beurteilen Sie, inwiefern folgende Kriterien auf das Reiseziel friesisches Wattenmeer zutreffen.

	trifft voll zu	trifft eher zu	trifft eher nicht zu	trifft überhaupt nicht zu	keine Angabe
gutes Preis-Leistungs-verhältnis	O	O	O	O	O
hohe Qualität der touristischen Leistungen	O	O	O	O	O
schöne Landschaft	O	O	O	O	O
historische und kulturelle Sehenswürdig-keiten	O	O	O	O	O
Möglichkeiten für Ausflüge und Unter-nehmungen	O	O	O	O	O
Einkaufs-möglichkeiten	O	O	O	O	O
Aktivitäten und Sport an der frischen Luft	O	O	O	O	O
gute Erreichbarkeit	O	O	O	O	O
Sicherheit	O	O	O	O	O
Kinder-freundlichkeit	O	O	O	O	O
viele Menschen/ hohes Touristen-aufkommen	O	O	O	O	O
freundliche Einwohner	O	O	O	O	O
entspannte Atmosphäre	O	O	O	O	O
behagliche Atmosphäre	O	O	O	O	O

10. Wie würden Sie auf einer Skala von 1 bis 4 das Reiseziel friesisches Wattenmeer beschreiben?

1= unangenehm, 2= eher unangenehm, 3= eher angenehm, 4= angenehm

unangenehm 1O 2O 3O 4O **angenehm** O keine Angabe

1= langweilig, 2= eher langweilig, 3= eher interessant, 4= interessant

langweilig 1O 2O 3O 4O **interessant** O keine Angabe

1= distanziert, 2= eher distanziert, 3= eher gastlich, 4= gastlich

distanziert 1O 2O 3O 4O **gastlich** O keine Angabe

1= vorhersehbar, 2= eher vorhersehbar, 3= eher überraschend, 4= überraschend

vorhersehbar 1O 2O 3O 4O **überraschend** O keine Angabe

1= schlicht, 2= eher schlicht, 3= eher luxuriös, 4= luxuriös

schlicht 1O 2O 3O 4O **luxuriös** O keine Angabe

1= einseitig, 2= eher einseitig, 3= eher abwechslungsreich, 4= abwechslungsreich

einseitig 1O 2O 3O 4O **abwechslungsreich** O keine Angabe

1= traditionell, 2= eher traditionell, 3= eher modern, 4= modern

traditionell 1O 2O 3O 4O **modern** O keine Angabe

11. Für wie einzigartig halten Sie folgende Eigenschaften des friesischen Wattenmeeres im Vergleich zu anderen Reisezielen in Küstenregionen?

	einzigartig	einigermaßen außergewöhnlich	gewöhnlich	überhaupt nicht außergewöhnlich	keine Angabe
das Watt	O	O	O	O	O
Küstenlandschaft	O	O	O	O	O
Marine Tier- und Pflanzenwelt	O	O	O	O	O
Platz und Weite	O	O	O	O	O
ruhige Umgebung	O	O	O	O	O
Insel-Gefühl	O	O	O	O	O
UNESCO-Welterbe	O	O	O	O	O
Mentalität der Einwohner	O	O	O	O	O

III Angaben zu Ihrer Person

Geschlecht: O weiblich O männlich

Wie alt sind Sie? _____ Jahre

Familienstand O ledig O in einer Partnerschaft lebend O verheiratet O geschieden O verwitwet

Haben Sie Kinder und wenn ja, wie viele? O nein O ja, Anzahl: _____

Welchen höchsten allgemeinbildenden Bildungsabschluss haben Sie?

O keinen
O Volks- oder Hauptschulabschluss
O mittlere Reife, Realschulabschluss o.ä.
O Fachhochschulreife, Abitur
O berufliche Ausbildung
O abgeschlossenes Studium

In welchem Bundesland leben Sie gegenwärtig?

O Baden-Württemberg
O Bayern
O Berlin
O Brandenburg
O Bremen
O Hamburg
O Hessen
O Mecklenburg-Vorpommern
O Niedersachsen
O Nordrhein-Westfalen
O Rheinland-Pfalz
O Saarland
O Sachsen
O Sachsen-Anhalt
O Schleswig-Holstein
O Thüringen

Vielen Dank für Ihre Teilnahme!

Online questionnaire

Fragebogen Image des Reiseziels friesisches Wattenmeer

Als Studentin des Internationalen Studienganges Tourismusmanagement an der Hochschule Bremen führe ich in Zusammenarbeit mit dem European Tourism Futures Institute in den Niederlanden eine Bachelorarbeit zum Thema Image des Reiseziels friesisches Wattenmeer durch.

Dies umfasst alle Vorstellungen, Gefühle und Bilder, die Sie mit dem Reiseziel friesisches Wattenmeer verbinden. Diese Region liegt im Nordwesten der Niederlande und erstreckt sich sowohl entlang der Küste der holländischen Provinz Friesland, sowie über die Westfriesischen Inseln Vieland, Terschelling, Ameland und Schiermonnikoog.

Im Rahmen dieses Projektes würde ich Sie bitten, einige Fragen über das genannte Reiseziel zu beantworten. Selbstverständlich werden Ihre Daten anonym verarbeitet. Bei Rückfragen oder Unklarheiten stehe ich Ihnen gerne zur Verfügung. Sie erreichen mich via E-mail: sschmaus@stud.hs-bremen.de.

Vielen Dank für Ihre Mitarbeit!

Reiseverhalten

1. Was ist Ihr liebstes Reiseziel in einer Küstenregion?

2. Haben Sie schon einmal eine Reise an das friesische Wattenmeer unternommen?

- ja
- nein (weiter bei Frage 4)

3. Wie oft haben Sie in den letzten drei Jahren das friesische Wattenmeer bereist?

4. Wie hoch ist die Wahrscheinlichkeit, dass Sie in den nächsten drei Jahren eine Reise an das friesische Wattenmeer unternehmen werden?

- sehr wahrscheinlich
- wahrscheinlich
- unwahrscheinlich
- sehr unwahrscheinlich

Reiseziel friesisches Wattenmeer

5. Welche Eigenschaften oder Bilder fallen Ihnen ein, wenn Sie an das Reiseziel friesisches Wattenmeer denken?

(gerne in Stichworten)

6. Wie würden Sie die Atmosphäre oder Stimmung, die Sie mit dem Reiseziel friesisches Wattenmeer verbinden, beschreiben?

(gerne in Stichworten)

7. Bitte nennen Sie charakteristische oder einzigartige Merkmale, die Sie mit dem friesischen Wattenmeer verbinden.

(gerne in Stichworten)

8. Bitte beurteilen Sie den Gesamteindruck, den Sie vom Reiseziel friesisches Wattenmeer haben.

- ○ positiv
- ○ eher positiv
- ○ eher negativ
- ○ negativ
- ○ keine Angabe

9. Bitte beurteilen Sie, inwiefern folgende Kriterien auf das friesische Wattenmeer zutreffen.

1= trifft voll zu, 2= trifft eher zu, 3= trifft eher nicht zu, 4= trifft überhaupt nicht zu

	1	2	3	4	keine Angabe
gutes Preis-Leistungsverhältnis	○	○	○	○	○
hohe Qualität der touristischen Leistungen	○	○	○	○	○
schöne Landschaft	○	○	○	○	○
historische und kulturelle Sehenswürdigkeiten	○	○	○	○	○
Möglichkeiten für Ausflüge und Unternehmungen	○	○	○	○	○
Einkaufsmöglichkeiten	○	○	○	○	○
Aktivitäten und Sport an der frischen Luft	○	○	○	○	○
gute Erreichbarkeit	○	○	○	○	○
Sicherheit	○	○	○	○	○
Kinderfreundlichkeit	○	○	○	○	○
viele Menschen/ hohes Touristenaufkommen	○	○	○	○	○
freundliche Einwohner	○	○	○	○	○
entspannte Atmosphäre	○	○	○	○	○
behagliche Atmosphäre	○	○	○	○	○

10. Wie würden Sie das Reiseziel friesisches Wattenmeer beschreiben?

○ unangenehm
○ eher unangenehm
○ eher angenehm
○ angenehm
○ keine Angabe

○ langweilig
○ eher langweilig
○ eher interessant
○ interessant
○ keine Angabe

- distanziert
- eher distanziert
- eher gastlich
- gastlich
- keine Angabe

- vorhersehbar
- eher vorhersehbar
- eher überraschend
- überraschend
- keine Angabe

- schlicht
- eher schlicht
- eher luxuriös
- luxuriös
- keine Angabe

- einseitig
- eher einseitig
- eher abwechslungsreich
- abwechslungsreich
- keine Angabe

- traditionell
- eher traditionell
- eher modern
- modern
- keine Angabe

11. Für wie einzigartig halten Sie folgende Eigenschaften des friesischen Wattenmeeres im Vergleich zu anderen Reisezielen in Küstenregionen?

1= einzigartig, 2= einigermaßen außergewöhnlich, 3= gewöhnlich, 4= überhaupt nicht außergewöhnlich

	1	2	3	4	keine Angabe
das Watt	○	○	○	○	○
die Küstenlandschaft	○	○	○	○	○
Marine Tier- und Pflanzenwelt	○	○	○	○	○
Platz und Weite	○	○	○	○	○
ruhige Umgebung	○	○	○	○	○
Insel-Gefühl	○	○	○	○	○
UNESCO-Welterbe	○	○	○	○	○
Mentalität der Einwohner	○	○	○	○	○

Angaben zu Ihrer Person

12. Geschlecht

○ weiblich
○ männlich

13. Alter

14. Familienstand

○ ledig
○ in einer Partnerschaft lebend
○ verheiratet
○ geschieden
○ verwitwet

15. Haben Sie Kinder?

○ ja
○ nein (weiter bei Frage 17)

16. Wieviele Kinder haben Sie?

17. Welchen höchsten allgemeinbildenden Bildungsabschluss haben Sie?

- ◯ keinen
- ◯ Volks- oder Hauptschulabschluss
- ◯ mittlere Reife, Realschulabschluss o.ä.
- ◯ Fachhochschulreife, Abitur
- ◯ berufliche Ausbildung
- ◯ abgeschlossenes Studium
- ◯ Sonstiges: ____________

18. In welchem Bundesland leben Sie gegenwärtig?

- ◯ Baden-Württemberg
- ◯ Bayern
- ◯ Berlin
- ◯ Brandenburg
- ◯ Bremen
- ◯ Hamburg
- ◯ Hessen
- ◯ Mecklenburg-Vorpommern
- ◯ Niedersachsen
- ◯ Nordrhein-Westfalen
- ◯ Rheinland-Pfalz
- ◯ Saarland
- ◯ Sachsen
- ◯ Sachsen-Anhalt
- ◯ Schleswig-Holstein
- ◯ Thüringen

Vielen Dank für Ihre Teilnahme!

2 Relationship tables

place of residence * overall image

		overall image				
place of residence		positive	rather positive	rather negative	negative	total
	Baden-Württemberg	3	2	2	1	8
	Bavaria	9	14	3	2	28
	Berlin	1	2	1	0	4
	Brandenburg	0	1	0	0	1
	Bremen	20	10	2	1	33
	Hamburg	2	2	0	0	4
	Hesse	4	1	0	0	5
	Lower Saxony	5	2	0	0	7
	North Rhine-Westphalia	35	13	2	1	51
	Rhineland-Palatinate	2	3	0	0	5
	Saxony	0	1	0	0	1
	Saxony-Anhalt	0	0	0	1	1
	Schleswig-Holstein	0	2	0	0	2
	total	81	53	10	6	150

place of residence * probability of visit

		probability of visit				
place of residence		very probable	probable	improbable	very improbable	total
	Baden-Württemberg	0	1	6	1	8
	Bavaria	2	8	18	4	32
	Berlin	1	0	2	1	4
	Brandenburg	0	0	1	0	1
	Bremen	13	9	10	2	34
	Hamburg	3	0	1	0	4
	Hesse	1	1	4	0	6
	Lower Saxony	4	2	1	0	7
	North Rhine-Westphalia	22	12	13	4	51
	Rhineland-Palatinate	2	0	3	0	5
	Saxony	0	1	0	2	3
	Saxony-Anhalt	0	0	1	0	1
	Schleswig-Holstein	0	0	1	0	1
	total	48	34	61	14	157

probability of visit * overall image

		overall image				
probability of visit		positive	rather positive	rather negative	negative	total
	very probable	39	9	0	0	48
	probable	18	15	0	0	33
	improbable	22	26	6	2	56
	very improbable	2	3	4	3	12
	total	81	53	10	5	149

visitation * probability of visit

		probability of visit				
visitation		very probable	probable	improbable	very improbable	total
	yes	45	23	25	3	96
	no	3	11	36	12	62
	total	48	34	61	15	158

age * visit

	visit			
age		yes	no	total
	20-24	19	21	40
	25-29	22	16	38
	30-34	5	2	7
	35-39	5	2	7
	40-44	2	1	3
	45-49	7	0	7
	50-54	11	6	17
	55-59	17	9	26
	60-64	5	5	10
	65-69	2	1	3
	70+	0	1	1
	total	95	64	159

family status * visitation

	visitation			
family status		yes	no	total
	single	30	31	61
	in a relationship	25	12	37
	married	33	18	51
	divorced	4	1	5
	widowed	4	2	6
	total	96	64	160

3 Mega data on German population

Gender (2010)		
	absolute numbers (1000)	share (%)
men	40,112,4	49.1
women	41,639,2	50.9
total	81,751,6	100

Age (2010)			
	absolute numbers (1000)	share (%)	weighted share (%)
15-25	9,136,4	11.2	12.9
25-45	21,387,6	26.2	30.2
45-65	23,442,2	28.9	33.1
65+	16,844,3	20.6	23.8

Family status (2010)		
	absolute numbers (1000)	share (%)
single	34,394,6	42.1
married	34,974,7	42.8
divorced/widowed	12, 382,3	15.1

Population per Federal State (2010)		
	absolute numbers (1000)	share (%)
Baden-Württemberg	10,753,880	13.3
Bayern	12,538,696	15.3
Berlin	3,460,725	4.2
Brandenburg	2,503,273	3.1
Bremen	660,706	0.81
Hamburg	1,786,448	2.2
Hessen	6,067,021	7.4
Mecklenburg-Vorpommern	1,642,327	2.0
Niedersachsen	7,918,293	9.7

Nordrhein-Westfalen	17,845,154	21.8
Rheinland-Pfalz	4,003,745	5.0
Saarland	1,017,567	1.2
Sachsen	4,149,477	5.1
Sachsen-Anhalt	2,335,006	2.9
Schleswig-Holstein	2,834,259	3.5
Thüringen	2,235,025	2.7
Deutschland	81,751,602	100

SCHRIFTENREIHE DER SCHOOL OF INTERNATIONAL BUSINESS
Internationaler Studiengang für Tourismusmanagement (ISTM)

Herausgegeben von Felix Bernhard Herle

ISSN 1863-9798

1 *Katharina Schirmbeck*
Markenbildung für Regionen
Dachmarkenkonzepte im deutschen Regionalmarketing
ISBN 3-89821-689-6

2 *Stefanie Kranawetter und Ivonne Mühlner*
Erfolgreiches Krisenmanagement für Reiseveranstalter
Ein Handbuch für plötzlich auftretende Krisen im Tourismus
ISBN 978-3-89821-835-1

3 *Angela Bergner*
Tourismus als Mittel zur Armutsminderung in Nepal
Das "Tourism for Rural Poverty Alleviation Programme" (TRPAP)
ISBN 978-3-89821-853-5

4 *Felix Bernhard Herle*
Strategische Planung grenzenloser Destinationen
Vertikale und branchenübergreifende Erweiterung Touristischer Regionen
ISBN 978-3-89821-908-2

5 *Birte Heidbreder*
Gütesiegel zur Einflussnahme auf die touristische Entwicklung einer Destination
Erfolgsanalyse des CST Costa Ricas für nachhaltigen Tourismus
ISBN 978-3-89821-986-0

6 *Linda von Nerée*
Das touristische Potential Hamburgs für chinesische Europa-Reisende
Eine Bestandsanalyse mit konkreten Veränderungsvorschlägen
ISBN 978-3-89821-780-4

7 *Joana Heinemann*
Mountainbike-Tourismus im Wettbewerb
Zielgruppenorientierte Optimierung von Packages im Destinationsmarketing
ISBN 978-3-8382-0167-2

8 *Tina Böttinger*
Die Entwicklung der Erlebnisorientierung
Status quo und Perspektiven in der Kreuzfahrt- und Themenparkbranche
ISBN 978-3-8382-0259-4

9 *Moritz Busch*
Kooperationspotenziale von Lufthansa und Germanwings aus Konsumentenperspektive
Eine Untersuchung zu Einflussfaktoren auf die konsumentenperspektivische Akzeptanz von Kooperationen konträrer Geschäftsmodelle
ISBN 978-3-8382-0456-7

10 *Stefanie Schmaus*
A Brand Identity for the Frisian Wadden Sea
Destination Branding on the Basis of Destination Image Analysis
ISBN 978-3-8382-0490-1

Abonnement

Hiermit abonniere ich die *Schriftenreihe der School of International Business – Internationaler Studiengang für Tourismusmanagement (ISTM)* **(ISSN 1863-9798),** herausgegeben von Felix Bernhard Herle,

❒ ab Band # 1

❒ ab Band # ___

❒ Außerdem bestelle ich folgende der bereits erschienenen Bände:

#___, ___, ___, ___, ___, ___, ___, ___, ___, ___, ___, ___

❒ ab der nächsten Neuerscheinung

❒ Außerdem bestelle ich folgende der bereits erschienenen Bände:

#___, ___, ___, ___, ___, ___, ___, ___, ___, ___, ___, ___

❒ 1 Ausgabe pro Band ODER ❒ ___ Ausgaben pro Band

Bitte senden Sie meine Bücher zur versandkostenfreien Lieferung innerhalb Deutschlands an folgende Anschrift:

Vorname, Name: ___________________________

Straße, Hausnr.: ___________________________

PLZ, Ort: ___________________________

Tel. (für Rückfragen): ______________ *Datum, Unterschrift:* ______________

Zahlungsart

❒ *ich möchte per Rechnung zahlen*

❒ *ich möchte per Lastschrift zahlen*

bei Zahlung per Lastschrift bitte ausfüllen:

Kontoinhaber: ___________________________

Kreditinstitut: ___________________________

Kontonummer: ______________ Bankleitzahl: ______________

Hiermit ermächtige ich jederzeit widerruflich den *ibidem*-Verlag, die fälligen Zahlungen für mein Abonnement der *Schriftenreihe der School of International Business – Internationaler Studiengang für Tourismusmanagement (ISTM)* von meinem oben genannten Konto per Lastschrift abzubuchen.

Datum, Unterschrift: ___________________________

Abonnementformular entweder **per Fax** senden an: **0511 / 262 2201** oder 0711 / 800 1889 oder als **Brief** an: *ibidem*-Verlag, Julius-Leber Weg 11, 30457 Hannover oder als **e-mail** an: **ibidem@ibidem-verlag.de**

***ibidem*-Verlag**
Melchiorstr. 15
D-70439 Stuttgart
info@ibidem-verlag.de

www.ibidem-verlag.de
www.ibidem.eu
www.edition-noema.de
www.autorenbetreuung.de

Zeitfracht Medien GmbH
Ferdinand-Jühlke-Straße 7
99095 Erfurt, Deutschland
produktsicherheit@kolibri360.de